Praise for *Mind Your Own Mortgage*

"Picking up a new mortgage isn't like shopping for shoes. It's more like entering into the competition of your life. . . . You need your own coach to win the mortgage game—someone who's on your side, fully aware of the competition's strategies and what's in their playbook; a coach who will walk with you through the transaction, explaining every move with clear and sound advice from start to finish. Whether you're getting a new mortgage, refinancing an old one, or dealing with the mortgage you have already, you won't find a better mortgage coach than my friend Rob Bernabé. The book you hold in your hands, *Mind Your Own Mortgage*, will bring him alongside with expert knowledge you can trust, passion that is genuine, and everything you need to play the mortgage game well. And come out victorious. Every time!"

— MARY HUNT
*personal finance expert and
best-selling author and CEO of
Debt-Proof Living*

"Rob is a consumer advocate in the greatest sense. He is an innovator and pioneer, having championed efforts to bring clarity and certainty to mortgage consumers at E*TRADE Financial. He piloted our mortgage business into the stratosphere by offering the first-of-its-kind guaranteed up-front pricing which eliminated guesswork and gave consumers a fair shake. *Mind Your Own Mortgage* reverse engineers Rob's vision from a business offering to a consumer-led revolution of the mortgage industry. Finally, consumers have what they need to hold any mortgage provider accountable—not to mention the tools needed to manage and pay off their mortgage debt."

— R. JARRETT LILIEN
*founder and managing partner
of Bendigo Partners and former
president and COO of E*TRADE
Financial*

"Wow. *Mind Your Own Mortgage* has the potential to dramatically change the mortgage lending landscape—provided you read and apply the material. Rob is a regular guest on my radio program, and through our relationship, I've come to realize there's a huge untold story—one that you must grasp in order to successfully navigate your mortgage debt from the time you obtain it to the day you kiss it good-bye. Rob's book lays it out for you—providing the prescription to go from beginning to end with no pain in between."

— FRANK PASTORE
The Frank Pastore Show,
Los Angeles, CA

"*Mind Your Own Mortgage* is a powerful work, combining time-tested and stalwart financial truths with a fresh approach to mortgage finance that will test everything you've been led to believe about your most significant debt. Take care to unpack the contents of this book. You'll find stored within solid guidance that will consist in making better informed choices in your personal financial journey."

— KENNY LUCK
CEO of Everyman Ministries,
Men's Pastor at Saddleback
Church, Lake Forest, CA, and
best-selling author

"In my time serving alongside Rob at Saddleback Church, I've watched Rob as he taught thousands of people the principles covered in *Mind Your Own Mortgage*. Follow the sound financial principles in this book and they will transform your life. Your mortgage is a critical component of your overall financial picture, and the consequences of getting it wrong can be severe. This book will help you get it right."

— CHRIS GOULARD
Pastor of Financial Stewardship,
Saddleback Church, Lake
Forest, CA

MIND
YOUR OWN
MORTGAGE

MIND
YOUR OWN
MORTGAGE

The **WISE HOME OWNER'S GUIDE** *to*
Choosing, Managing, *and* **Paying Off Your Mortgage**

Robert J. Bernabé

THOMAS NELSON
Since 1798

NASHVILLE   DALLAS   MEXICO CITY   RIO DE JANEIRO

Published in Nashville, Tennessee, by Thomas Nelson. Thomas Nelson is a registered trademark of Thomas Nelson, Inc.

Published in association with Rosenbaum & Associates Literary Agency, Brentwood, Tennessee.

Thomas Nelson, Inc., titles may be purchased in bulk for educational, business, fund-raising, or sales promotional use. For information, please e-mail SpecialMarkets@ ThomasNelson.com.

Library of Congress Cataloging-in-Publication Data

Bernabe, Robert, 1960–
    Mind your own mortgage : the wise home owner's guide to choosing, managing, and paying off your mortgage / Robert Bernabe.
       p. cm.
    ISBN 978-1-59555-088-0
    1. Mortgage loans—United States. 2. House buying—United States. I. Title.
HG2040.5.U5B475 2010
332.7'20973—dc22   2010000221

Printed in the United States of America

10 11 12 13 14 RRD 5 4 3 2 1

To my beautiful wife, whose faith and dedication to our family inspires me on a daily basis. I love you, honey! I thank God for granting me the honor to marry his daughter.

To anyone across America who recognizes their mortgage can make or break their financial dreams—and those who don't. This book was written expressly for you. If you absorb the content and put it into practice, you will discover a whole new way to manage your mortgage debt and gain new perspectives. You'll have the tools you need to take control and you'll be well on your way to that glorious day of being mortgage free.

To all those who have the courage to say no to excess consumerism and are ready to live a better life. You will build a strong household economy and together we will build a strong American economy.

Contents

INTRODUCTION

The New Deal

Simple, clear, and straightforward.

Wouldn't it be nice if the word *mortgage* brought these terms to mind?

If you feel helpless when it comes to shopping for a mortgage, you are not alone. Buying a mortgage isn't like finding the cheapest gallon of gas in town. You can't look at the sign on the mortgage storefront and make a determination. You have to walk inside the store and give up a pile of personal information. And what do you get in return? Instead of a simple quote, you are presented with a complicated list of fees and charges and confusing interest rate options. It's hard enough to extract information from one lender—try checking out more than one. Go ahead—walk inside each shop to obtain your quotes and then go figure out who's got the best deal. That's nearly impossible!

Think about this: money is a commodity. Mortgages are made of money. Isn't commodity pricing supposed to be simple? Is there any difference between a thirty-year fixed-rate mortgage from one lender to the next? There isn't. And correspondingly, that thirty-year mortgage is priced as a commodity throughout the entire supply chain . . . until it reaches you. Then things become convoluted to the point of being contrary to what they should be. Why, if things were the way they should be, mortgage companies would be forced to become transparent and compete on price. Here's the bottom line: simple, clear, and complete price information is *purposely* withheld to prevent a market where consumers can easily determine the best deal.

But in your hands lies a shopping system that will allow you to obtain the necessary information, so you can make the best choice the next time around. You are going to force commodity pricing so you can determine who has the best deal. You're going to shop for your mortgage like it's a gallon of gas!

Yet shopping is only part of the battle. You need to know when to engage. Instead of responding to the mortgage company's prod to refinance, you need a purposeful plan that tells you when to refinance and what to do with the monthly "savings" (a term that is wrongly associated with a reduction in monthly mortgage payments). Your strategy will be to refinance only when it makes good economic sense. Doing anything less is a waste of your time and a threat to your long-term financial health.

You also need to manage your debt while it's outstanding. Think of it this way: it isn't *your money* if you are in debt—your lender has a current and future claim on your cash and your time. Do you freely spend before you consider paying down your debts? Did you know paying down mortgage debt results in savings in the form of compounded and cancelled interest over the life of the mortgage—generating guaranteed returns as high as 600 percent? Will you be mortgage free when you retire, or will you have many years left to pay? How about getting there before retirement? Wouldn't that be nice?

It's Time to Think Differently

Your financial life begins and ends with your mortgage—it's your largest debt—so you must not limit your thinking to the check you cut each month. Too many of us are in economic trouble because we haven't been taught the correct way to think about home ownership and mortgage debt. Our society is swimming in debt to pay for a lifestyle that has ultimately become a trap. We are in the midst of a serious crisis, caused by credit that was supposed to enable the American Dream but instead has turned into a nightmare. Yes, the government and the credit industry must undertake serious change, but the fact remains that the American consumer is free to choose, and the choices we make carry consequences. Blaming those consequences on someone else isn't going to help anyone.

There remains the necessity to fundamentally change the way mortgage debt is handled. And this change must be led by the consumer. We must look to keeping our economic house in order. Each household must become financially viable—today and in the long run. You know the old saying: strong family, strong country. The same holds true for the economy: strong household economies, strong American economy. You might be one of the fortunate to have avoided economic woes brought on by mortgage debt, but you still need to look to a future that doesn't involve a mortgage. Does anything less make sense?

You must take control of your financial life by understanding the choices you have and making informed decisions. In order to own a home, unless you are sitting on a pile of money, you'll have to carry a mortgage. And in order to make informed decisions when it comes to that mortgage, you are going to have to go against the grain of some or all of what you've been taught.

It Doesn't Have to Be This Way

The housing meltdown that began in 2007—and its resulting economic consequences—gave rise to the realization that many of us held "toxic" mortgage debt. During the good times, economic circumstances can conceal the nasty truth about a mortgage, making it seem like things are just fine. The truth is, you are *always* in a potentially toxic financial situation—or not. What you need is the skill to recognize which is which, so you can get on the good side—and stay there—by managing the situation.

Most of us will have a mortgage for the majority of our adult lives. It's a long-term deal and you simply must understand how to actively manage your mortgage for the *entire time* it remains outstanding, or it has the propensity to become the beast so many of us are battling today.

Fortunately, managing your mortgage debt can be a straightforward process if you are dedicated to keeping things simple. You need to do three things in order to be successful:

1. Shop for a mortgage like it's a gallon of gas—treat it like a commodity and make it all about price, not payment.
2. Refinance only when it's beneficial to do so—when you can reduce the cost of your mortgage debt.
3. Manage your mortgage with the end in mind—an early payoff date.

In *Mind Your Own Mortgage*, you'll learn how to do all three, and when you are finished, you will be well on your way to that glorious day of becoming mortgage free.

It's about time for the New Deal—but this time, *we're* going to do it. Read on.

GET A GRIP
ON IT

1

WHAT'S WRONG?

The Profit Motive

Every business is motivated by the need to make a profit. Naturally, the profit motive can compete with the consumer's best interests. That doesn't make a business "the bad guy"—no one is holding a gun to your head to make you buy anything. It just means you need to be an astute consumer by realizing there is a profit motive and your money is the source of the profit.

As a home owner, you are therefore a reasonable and justifiable target in the open market: someone's going to try to sell you a mortgage whenever it makes business sense to make the pitch. And it's the pitch that sets up the obstacles, which prevent you from eliminating your mortgage debt:

The shopping focus is directed to payment rather than price.

Buying anything on time—making payments—is going to cost you more than paying cash. Some things, like a home, make sense to buy on time. The problem is mortgages are sold to you based on how much you want your monthly payment to be, rather than how much the mortgage will cost you. The shift from price to payment, combined with a lack of tools to make comparison shopping easy, sets you up for overcharges that can cost tens of thousands over the life of the loan—and even fool you into taking the wrong loan at the worst possible time.

Before you buy a home or refinance your existing mortgage, you must understand the total cost of your mortgage. You must understand *price*—how to extract it when shopping and how to compare quotes from multiple lenders—before you commit to borrow. Doing anything less is asking for big trouble.

The mortgage industry is designed to enslave home owners to perpetual debt.

Mortgage providers make money by writing mortgages. It is therefore in their best interests to refinance your mortgage debt over and over again with never-ending promises of lower payments. If you are mortgage free, how are they going to make money?

Most home owners don't actively manage their mortgage debt.

A mortgage finances your most significant asset and constitutes your largest debt. Therefore, how you manage it has a dramatic impact on your financial future. Do it right, and it leads to the elimination of mortgage debt; get it wrong and it can lead you into slavery to your mortgage.

People who mismanage their mortgage usually fall prey to one of two things. First, they spend their discretionary income instead of paying down their debt. Each time a home owner decides to spend rather than to invest by paying down mortgage debt, the household forgoes the opportunity to cancel thousands of dollars of future interest and to accelerate the mortgage payoff date. Spending costs money and over time it costs you the opportunity to become mortgage free. If you spend today, you'll trade tomorrow away.

Second, they become serial refinancers. The typical home owners who do this will refinance many times over, believing they are saving money by lowering their payment, unaware that each refinance costs more in the long run than the monthly payment savings.

Removing the Obstacles

A common theme among the obstacles to personal financial health is your mortgage payment. To correct what's wrong, you have to ignore the payment pitch. You must frame mortgage debt within the parameters of price when you shop for it and the cost of carrying it once you've obtained it.

Your next task is to tackle paying off your mortgage. Your mortgage may seem like a mountain, but mountains can be moved. You can start a pebble at a time and your efforts will automatically multiply. Before you know it, you'll be pulling down boulders the size of houses.

2

MIND YOUR OWN
MORTGAGE!

Joe and Linda:
It's Just Another Payment

The mailer said they could save up to $500 per month by refinancing their mortgage. Joe, 34, and Linda, 32, decided to give the mortgage company a call and, after taking a look at their mortgage quote, decided to proceed. They didn't see the need to shop around, since the new rate sounded good and it turned out they were going to save $425 a month.

Not long after they refinanced, things returned to normal. They hardly had any money left at the end of the month but they were always able to pay their bills. Neither of them gave a thought as to how their finances had changed. The reality was the extra $425 sort of evaporated into their monthly expenses—they haven't saved a dime since refinancing. As a matter of fact, they don't think about it: the word *savings* doesn't enter their minds and neither does the payoff date of their mortgage. They just make the monthly payment and leave it at that.

In the future lies the toxic truth: their new mortgage payoff date is seven years later than the original and that $425 "savings" is being borrowed against tomorrow.

It's just another payment. Nothing more. And it's costing them dearly.

Your mortgage should facilitate the American Dream. It's what you use to acquire a home, which functions as much more than just shelter—it's the base from which you conduct your life. But the American Dream is only rented until the day you become mortgage free. What most people don't realize is it's simple to accomplish this, as long as you don't abuse debt. Unlike virtually all other debt, mortgage debt finances an asset that appreciates over time. Because of this and other unique features of your mortgage, what you do with this debt has a dramatic impact on your financial future.

No One Is Going to Do It for You

There's a lot of reform going on in the mortgage industry. There are bailouts and government-sponsored loan modification programs that would have never been necessary had we properly managed our mortgage debt as a society.

So if you want to avoid trouble, you will be well served neither to rely on the integrity of the mortgage industry nor to have faith in the government to protect your interests. You must acquire the requisite knowledge and use it to protect your finances. In your life, money is one of the things over which you must assume ownership and accept responsibility. Proper stewardship begins with you.

Unfortunately, mortgages are delivered through a system that will trap you in perpetual debt if you allow yourself to be caught off guard. The very fiber and economic structure of the mortgage industry, combined with certain cultural forces, is designed to keep you coming back for more.

Mortgage providers all are competing for your business, and they rely on you to refinance your mortgage many times over. It is a requirement for their survival to have you come back to the well for a drink over and over again. This should be your first clue to be on guard. While there are good reasons to refinance your mortgage debt, they are limited and are far outnumbered by the reasons the industry uses to coax you into a new loan.

Do you allow the mortgage industry to lead you around by the nose, telling you when it's in your best interests to refinance? Whose interests do you think are being served?

Keep 'Em Coming Back

It's all too easy to lure you in and hook you up with a new mortgage. The primary bait is a lower payment. Who isn't interested in lowering their payments? You can accomplish this by lowering your rate through a simple refinance of your current mortgage, extending the term of your existing mortgage by writing a new one, or consolidating your higher rate loans into a new mortgage.

A lower payment is not a good reason to refinance. You have to look at it in the context of the overall picture, including the type of loan, the total cost of obtaining the new loan, the purpose of the refinance, your plan for the monthly savings that will be generated, and the long-term financial picture of your household. Certainly a lower payment alone isn't a great deal if you paid too much to acquire that payment. Nor is it a great deal if you end up with a loan that is subject to future increases. Let's say you obtained a great loan at the right price. Good for you! But if you don't have a plan to properly deal with the cash generated by the monthly payment reductions—or the discipline to stick to a plan—you will spend much more money in the long run than if you hadn't refinanced in the first place. Simply stated: a lower payment doesn't result in savings if you spend all of the savings!

A lower payment doesn't result in savings if you spend all of the savings!

Take a moment to listen carefully to the next mortgage radio ad you hear. Mortgage industry participants are constantly attempting to sell you a new, lower payment. This remarketing of mortgage debt aims to capture you numerous times over your life, and it will slowly tear away at your finances. The sad thing is, most people fall for the lower payment story—over and over again. Each time you refinance, you sign up for another thirty years of payments. And this is the crux of the problem.

To illustrate, let's look at an example. Let's assume you borrowed $350,000 to buy your home at a thirty-year fixed rate of 6.5 percent.

Five years later, interest rates have decreased, and one day you receive a notice in the mail about how you can save hundreds per month by refinancing your mortgage. Interested by the notice, you call the mortgage company that afternoon, and you find that you can refinance at a new rate of 6 percent, bringing your monthly payment from $2,212 down to $1,964. That's a monthly savings of $248, right? Wrong! The problem is your existing loan will be paid off in twenty-five years, and you're about to sign up for another thirty years, thereby adding another five years to your payment schedule.

So despite the fact that you've lowered your interest rate by a full 0.5 percent, you aren't going to save a dime in the long run. Sure, you'll have an extra $248 to spend each month, but because you added five years to your mortgage debt, you'll spend more than *$44,000* in additional interest on your new loan! How can this be? It's because the extension of the payoff date into the future causes interest charges that exceed the benefit of the reduction in your payment.

This is where sound financial planning and culture collide. Sound financial planning says, "Invest the $248 monthly savings wisely" and the culture says, "Spend it on whatever you want." If you do the latter, you'll have nothing to show for what could otherwise have been a sound financial decision. You see, things might look good to you at the moment of your decision to refinance, but the monthly cash flow savings don't matter much if you are forty-five years old and you haven't planned how you'll make the mortgage payment when you are seventy (with five years still left to go!).

You can see from the example above why the mortgage industry is going to pound on you to refinance any time it can lower your payment—it's an easy sell. Most of the time, it's not going to be a wise choice to go along.

More about adjustable-rate mortgages later, but for now just keep in mind they're another favorite bit of bait from the mortgage industry. It doesn't make sense to give up the security of a fixed-rate loan to refinance into the temporary lower payments of an adjustable-rate mortgage. If the interest rate market is at the point that refinancing makes sense, there will be a new fixed-rate loan available that will provide you with real benefits. The short-term benefit of lower payments (sold to you by the mortgage industry), when not weighed against a long-term view, can lead to significant troubles down the road.

Charge 'Em for the Pleasure

Unfortunately, the industry doesn't provide you with a clear picture to help you make good choices. There are a dizzying array of providers and mortgage products. Worse yet, there is little price transparency, making it very difficult to discern who's giving you the best (or at least a fair) deal.

The price you pay for any product or service is designed to maximize the profit to the business selling you the product or service. After all, they're in business to make money. It follows that you would be at greater risk of paying too much if little transparency exists. But there's more at work against you than just complexity and lack of transparency, and it comes in human form: the commissioned salesperson. More often than not, your loan officer or mortgage broker makes money in the form of a percentage of the revenue generated by the loan. He is thereby motivated to maximize the price for his own benefit. All too often, he is in control of the pricing you obtain, and if he can limit the amount of information you have, you are probably going to line his pockets.

Defend Yourself

All of this means you must constantly be aware of the need to properly mind your mortgage debt. If you are unaware of the proper circumstances under which you should refinance, do not understand the cost of doing so, don't know how your mortgage salesperson is compensated, don't know how to shop around, and don't have a plan to manage your mortgage debt over time, you are at great risk of paying too much, getting into the wrong loan, and causing yourself financial grief down the road. Add the fact the industry wants to keep you coming back for more, and you'll most likely make the same mistakes time and time again.

> *You need to understand what today's spending and borrowing decisions mean years from now.*

Defending yourself isn't just about understanding how to shop and avoid getting ripped off. The harder part will be taking a long-term view of home ownership and your related mortgage debt. You need to understand what today's spending and borrowing decisions mean years from now.

For example, let's say you have an extra $1,200 and you are considering buying a high-definition television. Is that television actually going to cost only $1,200? Let's paint a rosy picture and assume you are doing a good job saving for retirement, so you shell out $1,200 for the high-def TV. Was it a wise move? If you have mortgage debt, the answer is a resounding *no*. If you spend this money, you are essentially borrowing against your mortgage to do it. You'll end up with a television that is worthless five years from now and a mortgage for decades to come as you continue to consume rather than to pay down debt.

What is the long-term impact of this choice?

Let's say you forgo the TV and decide instead to pay down your mortgage by $1,200. If you are in year three of a $300,000 thirty-year loan at 6 percent, you'll *eliminate* approximately $5,000 of interest over the life of your loan. That's a guaranteed 417 percent return on your money!

Can you see how taking a long-term view would dramatically change your spending and borrowing decisions? In this example, you have some interesting choices. You can end up with a worthless television set, or save $5,000 and pay off your mortgage earlier.

Being wise with your cash isn't just about the high-definition television set. Whether it's an extra $50 or $1,200, these types of spending decisions come up month after month after month! This is where things start to add up and discipline will pay off. Each month you dedicate money to paying down your mortgage instead of spending it, you cancel future interest charges and get closer to the date you'll be mortgage free.

Albert Einstein is believed by some to have said compound interest "is the greatest mathematical discovery of all time." Whether he said it or not isn't the issue—it's the fact that a concept much simpler than $E=mc^2$ can have such a dramatic impact on the world. While compounding interest is normally associated with investing, it is equally true with mortgage debt: principal payments made in advance have a compounding effect on interest savings and the acceleration of the mortgage payoff date. If you pay down your debt rather than consume, the financial benefits of choosing the former are staggering. You'll see exactly how this works in a later chapter and you'll be given access to the tools to determine mortgage interest savings and monitor the accelerated payoff date in real time, month after month.

Instant gratification is your enemy, and a slow and steady pace is your friend. Because your mortgage payment doesn't decrease when you make additional payments, you can't immediately see the fruits of your labor. It takes time. It takes a slow and steady pace that multiplies down the road. In contrast, spending looms with the promise of tangible possessions, instantly gratifying yet destructive in the long run. Remember: the tortoise won the race against the hare.

Your frame of mind will dictate your success or failure in managing your mortgage debt. It is the single most important factor, yet it is the most difficult to control of all the variables that are involved in managing your debt. This is because there is an overriding propensity and temptation to spend, rather than to save or invest. Your discretionary dollars are up for grabs and an endless host of parties are after them—spurred by the media, advertising agencies, the credit industry, and even the government, who collectively and relentlessly hammer on you to consume rather than build your financial future. If you can resist these messages by applying your mind-set to a long-term view of your finances, you'll find some wonderful results:

- It becomes easier to resist spending as your savings accumulate or your mortgage debt pays down.
- You begin to see clearly a day when you won't be beholden to your mortgage payment.
- You become more resistant to the urge to borrow as you become freer to spend your time as you wish, rather than constantly spending your time making sure you can make ends meet.
- Your time becomes more available for the important people in your life, which you'll find to be more valuable than anything you could have purchased.

Let's Get Serious

Think about all the things you've purchased with credit in your life. Now look at your monthly payments. Does the pleasure provided by the things you've acquired outweigh the burden of the monthly payments you've signed up for? If the possessions are worth it, you should consider it a joyous occasion to make those payments each month! But I haven't met anybody who has accumulated a mountain of debt who has not regretted it.

Does the pleasure provided by the things you've acquired outweigh the burden of the monthly payments you've signed up for?

Once the debts pile up, you can either pay them off or you can lower the payments by extending into the future what is already inevitable: the eventual certainty that you must pay these debts. That sounds like slavery, but this is *exactly* where the credit industry wants you—to the point that you *must* come back for more, beholden to your debts. Don't do it! Stop consuming now and make a plan for getting out from under your debts.

The antithesis of slavery is freedom. I don't know about you, but my definition of freedom is being able to spend the time I've been given to fulfill my purpose in life. The culture would have you believe that one of the primary purposes of life is to acquire riches. Unfortunately, our culture has defined riches in the context of possessions and pleasures, which lead to the acquisition of debt—and slavery to it. This creates ideas like:

- I want that bigger house. I can see myself living in it and putting in a pool and a state-of-the-art entertainment center. I can afford the payments.
- My house has $100,000 in equity. If I buy that boat, I'll have so much fun with it—cruising along and basking in the sun

anchored in some brilliant bay. I can refinance to get the cash. I can afford the payments.

- We need to go on that big-time vacation. It'll be a great escape to get away from everything at work and at home. Our house has $50,000 in equity. We can use the cash to go on vacation, with a lot left over to refurnish our home. We can afford the payments.

- We need a second home. It would be nice not to have to pay to stay in someone else's place. It would be good to have a place to get away from it all. We can afford the payments.

Getting away from it all? Right!

This book isn't about your purpose in life. Far from it. However, there is a definite link from the culture to your mind-set and how you manage your finances. I'm suggesting that you need to break this link by redefining riches and what is important in life. Riches defined in the context of *relationships* are eternally more valuable than riches defined in the context of *things*. The culture will sell you hard on the latter, but when you really think about it, we all dream more of having more time to spend with our families and friends than most other things. Your mind-set toward riches, therefore, will define your desires, which will in turn drive how you spend your money, what you accomplish financially, and, ultimately, how you spend your time.

The primary purpose of this book is to help you take control, extract yourself from the culture, get to the point where your mortgage is a breeze, and free you up to concentrate on more important things in life. The United States is about three thousand miles wide from coast to coast, but we're about an inch deep when it comes to how we mind our mortgage debt. We're going to change this!

> *Minding your own mortgage, rather than allowing the industry and culture to mind it for you, will put you in a place far, far away from the painful reality that so many are living right now.*

Minding your own mortgage, rather than allowing the industry and culture to mind it for you, will put you in a place far, far away from the painful reality that so many are living right now. And it's going to prevent your future from becoming toxic—once and for all.

With this thought in mind, let's move on. Before we dive into the details of shopping for and managing mortgage debt, we briefly need to lay a foundation. It will help you to understand the basic workings of the mortgage market, how money makes its way from the source to you as a consumer, and to gain a general understanding of what led to the current credit crisis—for it is in the current credit crisis where the most valuable lessons lie.

3

THE MORTGAGE MARKET

Janie's Mortgage Broker

Janie owns a nice condo she bought ten years ago. The broker who helped her obtain the loan to buy her place has taken care of her mortgage needs ever since. She's refinanced a couple of times, each time lowering the payment and her interest rate.

Janie always looks for the best deal. She shops the grocery stores with the best weekly specials and refreshes her wardrobe only during her favorite store's semiannual sale. She drove a hard bargain when she bought her convertible last year and she shopped online to find the best price on airline tickets when she flew back East to visit her mother in the summer.

But Janie never shopped her mortgage. It didn't enter her mind—the mortgage broker's always been there for her and the process has been painless. How is it that Janie shops around for everything other than the largest financial transaction in her life? How does she know her broker is giving her a great deal?

She doesn't.

Money finds its way to your mortgage through a series of parties that collectively provide the funds necessary to service the nation's appetite for housing. Aside from the current credit crunch, liquidity has generally been made available to fuel what is still—by world standards—a relatively efficient housing market.

The Money Flow

You can think of the primary mortgage market like buying a product wholesale rather than retail—it's directly from the source.

At one end of the spectrum are investors who supply the capital needed to make mortgage loans and at the other end is the consumer—you—who fuels the mortgage market with home purchases and refinancing.

Let's take a look at the two most common ways loans flow to the consumer in the next chart.

Mortgages delivered by way of the consumer-direct flow are mortgages that are delivered by the primary mortgage market. You can think of the primary mortgage market as being like buying a product wholesale rather than retail—it's directly from the source.

The Consumer-Direct Flow

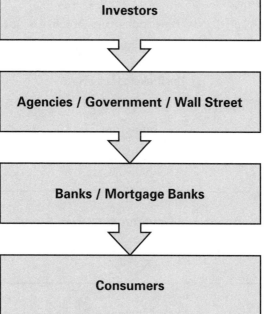

The primary mortgage market consists of lenders, which include banks, savings and loan institutions, credit unions, community banks, mortgage banking companies, and state and local housing finance agencies. These lenders have direct access to the funds necessary to make mortgage loans. Since they assume underwriting responsibility (determining the circumstances under which to lend money), they therefore control the credit decision. They may sell the loans they originate to investors, either through an agency or Wall Street, or they may retain the mortgages they originate for their own account. These lenders, along with the industry participants they sell loans to, are the entities that create the different loan products offered in the marketplace. Primary mortgage market lenders commonly refer to this as consumer-direct lending or retail lending.

The brokered loan flow looks very much like the consumer-direct flow, except it is one step removed from the money:

The Brokered Loan Flow

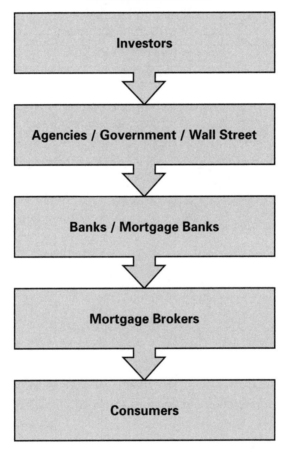

Mortgage brokers (intermediaries) serve as an interface between the primary mortgage market (lenders) and the consumer. Mortgage brokers are not lenders and therefore have no control over credit decisions, nor do they have access to the capital necessary to fund mortgage loans. Brokers usually align themselves with a number of primary mortgage market lenders, thereby offering their products at a markup from the prices the lenders give the broker. Brokers take mortgage applications, submit them for approval from a lender, and communicate with the borrower during the lending process until the loan is funded.

You can think of a mortgage broker as the sales end of the lender, acting as an agent for the lender rather than being directly employed by the lender. Economically, this allows the lender to acquire loans without advertising, relying on mortgage brokers to secure qualified customers.

Three Parts to a Mortgage Loan

1. The transaction
Writing a mortgage generates one-time fees for providing the lending or brokering service.

2. Interest charges
The holder of the mortgage charges interest based upon the terms of the mortgage.

3. Collecting payments
Because mortgages are commonly sold to investors, and most investors wish to collect interest on their money without having to collect

payments from borrowers, *mortgage servicing companies* collect the payment on behalf of the investor for a fee.

As loans are funded by banks and mortgage banks, they are either held in the lender's portfolio or they are packaged and sold in the *secondary mortgage market.* At this point, the mortgage begins to be pulled apart into its pieces—the lender retains the transaction income, sells the principal balance of your loan to another party who collects the interest, and sells the right to collect the payments. By selling loans in the secondary market, lenders are able to replenish the funds necessary to originate additional mortgage loans.

> *By selling loans in the secondary market, lenders are able to replenish the funds necessary to originate additional mortgage loans.*

The secondary mortgage market provides the great majority of funds that make mortgages possible. Mortgages sold in the secondary market are generally referred to as either *agency* or *nonagency loans.*

Agency loans are those loans that are underwritten to standards created by the formerly government-sponsored—and now government-owned—entities such as Fannie Mae or Freddie Mac. These loans are also commonly called conforming loans, because they conform to agency standards. Conforming loans are sold by lenders to the agencies, who in turn pool the loans and offer them for sale to investors, either directly or through brokerage houses on Wall Street. Agencies play a vital role in the nation's housing finance system by providing liquidity for lending operations in a variety of economic conditions.

While the housing meltdown led to a government takeover of these agencies, they have always been quasi-government entities. This is because the government steps in, when necessary, to ensure adequate liquidity exists in the financial system to fund mortgage loans. These agencies will likely continue to exist, in one form or another, as the economy takes shape in the years to come.

Nonagency loans are simply loans that do not conform to agency standards. These loans are made to underwriting standards that are acceptable to an investor, or are appropriate for the loan portfolio of a lending institution, such as a bank. The most commonly recognized nonagency loan is the *jumbo loan*, which is larger than the maximum loan size an agency will accept. In recent years, the most famous (or infamous) type of nonagency loan has been the *subprime loan*. Nonagency loans are most often sold to investors via brokerage houses on Wall Street. Examples of these types of loans are stated-income loans, option ARMs (or pick-a-pay loans), and a variety of other loan products that no longer exist and—as you will discover if you haven't already—were the seeds that gave rise to the foreclosure harvest.

The range of nonagency mortgage products available at any time is dependent upon general economic conditions, the health of the housing market, and the appetite of investors for instruments that are backed by mortgages. Beginning in 2007, degradation in each of these factors gave rise to an ever-shrinking pool of funds available to write mortgages. As the housing crisis continued to form, the liquidity continued to tighten. This tightening is a natural part of the economic cycle. The impact of this is covered in greater detail in the next chapter.

Investors of agency and nonagency loans include, but are not limited to, insurance companies, pension funds, commercial banks, fund managers, foreign banks, and other financial institutions.

In summary, consumers deal with intermediaries, such as brokers, or directly with lenders, who sell their loans to agencies or Wall Street—who in turn package the loans for sale to investors.

A Once-Fragmented Market Consolidates

Because the mortgage market is so large and lending laws vary from state to state (and sometimes from county to county or city to city), it is fragmented into a large number of players who operate at local, regional, and national levels. But fragmentation isn't driven solely by the size of the market and regulation. The mortgage market normally has very low barriers to entry, so in times of housing prosperity, new mortgage companies pop up like weeds. The low barriers also allow for a general lack of sophistication in the primary mortgage market; more so with mortgage brokers than with direct lenders, since it's much easier to set up a broker shop than to become a direct lender.

In times of housing prosperity, new mortgage companies pop up like weeds.

During the boom times, it was frightening how little knowledge most mortgage business owners had of the workings and economics of the mortgage market. It was all too easy to slap together a business, hire some salespeople, and hit the ground running. Fragmentation, primarily fueled by how easy it is to get into the business, is the major reason for the lack of price transparency, clarity, simplicity, and consistency in the mortgage product offering and process.

The lowest barrier of entry to the mortgage market is to become a mortgage broker. Statistically, even before the mortgage meltdown, brokered mortgage loans experience a higher rate of delinquency and default than mortgage loans written by direct lenders. This is due to the fact that lenders have less control over the relationship with the borrower, since the broker controls this relationship. As the economic crisis worsened, direct lenders began to sever relationships with brokers at a breakneck pace and the ones that were left became subject to more scrutiny than was exercised during boom times.

The mortgage meltdown resulted in a massive exit of industry players, most of which went belly-up, resulting in consolidation of the market. While the previously low barriers to entry allowed for a lack of sophistication and a wide range of practices aimed at selling mortgage products from any angle possible other than price, the remaining players have done little to correct the problems that give rise to bad decisions on the part of the consumer (except for the removal of toxic mortgage products from the market). There remains little movement on the part of the industry toward price clarity, certainty, or simplicity, since the economic benefits of avoiding clarity continue to outweigh the benefits of coming clean.

There remains little movement on the part of the industry toward price clarity, certainty, or simplicity, since the economic benefits of avoiding clarity continue to outweigh the benefits of coming clean.

Mortgage Broker or Direct Lender?

A common question asked by consumers is whether it's better to use a mortgage broker or direct lender. The truth is a direct lender is one step closer to the source of money for your mortgage—the secondary market. Direct lenders also make the underwriting and lending decisions, whereas brokers do not. Hence, a direct lender is normally a more efficient source for your mortgage, and correspondingly should be able to offer you a better price than a mortgage broker.

Mortgage brokers normally pride themselves on personal service and theoretically a wider variety of loan products, since they tend to broker their loans with several direct lenders. This advantage is greatly overstated and does not supply the value brokers usually claim to possess, particularly for borrowers with great credit histories. From a price standpoint, there are certain situations in which a mortgage broker may be able to offer a better price than a direct lender, but you won't know that until you know how to shop. Generally speaking, whether you are buying a mortgage or any other product, it's better to deal directly with the source than to work through a middleman. I know that statement is going to cause some huffing and puffing on behalf of the mortgage brokers out there, but it's the truth.

Prove it to yourself when you go out to shop for your next mortgage. When it comes to price, the question of using a mortgage broker or direct lender will be easily solved by applying the shopping system outlined herein. This system will reveal who has the best price, making your choice clear and eliminating the need for a long discourse on whether it's better to use a direct lender or a mortgage broker.

4

THE CREDIT CRISIS

Josh and Cheryl:
Squeezing into Their Home Squeezed Them Out of It

Josh and Cheryl didn't have the best credit history in the world and didn't have much savings in the bank. They wanted to buy a home and found a nice three-bedroom on the upper east side of their hometown. When they found they could qualify for the home, they were thrilled. The loan had a payment they could swing; they were able to obtain the home with little money down and a loan from Cheryl's uncle.

Josh and Cheryl didn't think of themselves as subprime, but their mortgage made them so. After two years of living in the home, their payments started to go up. By the third year, it became very difficult to make ends meet from month to month. But the home had risen in value and one day a mortgage lender called with a great offer at just the right time. They could refinance into a new loan that had fixed payments for two years, just like the one they'd started with. Having no other option, Josh and Cheryl went for it, adding another $10,000 to their mortgage in the process.

A few years later, payment shock hit them again. But this time, the value of their home had decreased slightly. This time no one called them. And no one they called could help them. As the payments continued to escalate, they began to fall behind. With nowhere to turn and the news blasting about the subprime mortgage market melting away, they realized the spot they were in.

Josh and Cheryl were standing at the edge of the abyss, with an untold number of folks coming right behind them. It was the summer of 2007, and several months later, they were squeezed out of the home they had squeezed into.

We learn valuable life lessons in the event of a crisis. The credit crisis that began in 2007 is no different in this respect. There are a lot of folks looking for someone to blame for the woes we are experiencing today, and there are several parties among which the blame can easily be assigned. But there's no use in assigning blame. What is going to help is to understand how this mess came about and the role the consumer played in contributing to it.

Any intense run-up in prices, whether it is housing, stocks, or oil, is unsustainable and creates a bubble that will burst.

The truth is, lessons were being taught all along the way; we just had very few students willing to listen until the crisis hit. Any intense run-up in prices, whether it is housing, stocks, or oil, is unsustainable and creates a bubble that will burst. The markets and greed will, at times, push prices beyond the point that they are reasonable. History has proven this to be true time and time again. The run-up in housing prices up until 2006 falls squarely within this definition. It was a purely temporary situation, driven by interest rates at forty-year lows and highly liquid credit markets.

Unsustainable Economies

Your home is financed by a thirty-year instrument called a mortgage. During that time, you will experience a variety of economic cycles, some of which will be significant to the upside and others severe to the downside. This doesn't take into account your personal life, which can be turned on a dime by the loss of a job, sickness, or a variety of other factors. Given the mortgage payment is your largest expense, you and your mortgage must work together if you are going to survive for thirty years.

Temporary market conditions can have a dramatic impact on your chances for survival. The forty-year-low interest rate cycle that lasted from 2001 to 2006 serves as a perfect example of a mortal threat. As housing prices continued to skyrocket, adjustable-rate mortgages were increasingly used to squeeze people into homes or to lower the monthly payments for existing home owners. This further fueled housing prices, causing further exposure to the eventual decline.

Anyone who bought into an adjustable-rate mortgage was either blind to the fact that interest rates would eventually rise off forty-year lows, or they ignored it. Low mortgage payments provided cash to consume, which helped fuel the general economy. And as house prices increased, consumer spending on large ticket items exploded as the number of mortgagees tapping rising home equity increased. Many consumers were spending far beyond their means—at unprecedented levels as they mortgaged their futures against their homes.

Housing, from the standpoint of interest rates and adjustable-rate mortgages, was therefore affordable only on a temporary basis: for as long as rates stayed low. The unsustainable household economy was well underway, the home mortgaged to the hilt and the family living as though the mortgage payment would never increase, leaving little or no margin for error. These unsustainable household economies were bound to crash the minute interest rates ticked upward. Rack up enough of these fatalities, and you have an unsustainable national economy.

Like it or not, highly leveraged financing will never work at the consumer level. Consumers, unlike businesses and investors, don't have the sophistication to create a hedge against changing economic circumstances. In stock trading, there's something named a margin call. Certain investors can buy stock on margin, which means they can borrow from the brokerage firm to buy a stock so long as they have invested their own money in the same stock. A margin call occurs when the price of the stock falls and the stock trader is required to make a deposit in order to cover the loss on the borrowed funds. If the amount cannot be covered, the brokerage will automatically sell enough stock to pay back the loan. While leverage was used to buy the stock in the first place, it is also used to force the trader out to avoid disaster (at least for the brokerage).

This isn't true with mortgage and consumer debt: you are allowed to continue to take risk as long as you continue to make your payments. There's no margin call to force you out before things get ugly. If it gets really bad, the lender is the one that will take it in the shorts when the home owner walks from a home that's worth less than he owes on it.

This time it's become so bad that we all took it in the shorts.

The Makings of a Perfect Storm

People began to talk about the return to a better economy as the credit crunch unfolded, along with the ensuing recession. Truth be told, we were already in a bad economy by 2004, long before the crash. Things looked good back then, but the American household (the primary source that fuels our economy) was leveraged to the point of becoming unsustainable—maxed out on the mortgage, car loans, and credit cards, with little or no savings. Consumer spending, facilitated by credit, does not a good economy make!

It's always the calm before the storm that fools you into believing things are going fine. Unsustainable household economies eventually lead to an unsustainable national economy—the making of a perfect storm, which would slam onto the beachhead of our nation in 2007 and wreak unprecedented havoc in the housing markets and the general economy.

Unsustainable household economies eventually lead to an unsustainable national economy.

To understand the development of the conditions that led to this credit crisis, we need to go back to the late 1980s, when subprime mortgages were introduced. At that time, there was a large population of borrowers who were underserved because of poor credit ratings; they had little or no access to mortgage loans. Charging a higher interest rate to such a borrower does not normally compensate for the risk of default. If the borrower doesn't pay up, there has to be a fallback position. The answer lies in home equity—as long as the lender limits the amount borrowed against the value of the home, a foreclosure takes care of everything. The mortgage industry refers to the ratio of the loan amount to the value of the home as *loan to the value* (or LTV). The LTV on subprime loans in those early days was typically no more than 70 percent. At these ratios, it can make business sense to loan money to a person with a low credit score.

Because the low LTV requirements would require large down payments, not many loans were made for the purpose of purchasing a home. However, a robust refinance market was created, serving borrowers whose credit scores had degraded since originally obtaining a mortgage. Lending to these borrowers was prudent. For example, assume a borrower whose credit was once A-grade loses a job or has a health issue that results in getting behind in his mortgage payments for a period of time—his credit score is trashed, but he has a large amount of home equity. When it comes time to refinance, the lender isn't concerned with the poor credit score because he can foreclose on the home in the event the borrower doesn't make the payments. In other words, subprime mortgages worked for the lender (because there was safety in home equity), and it worked for the borrower (because there was nowhere else to go to obtain a mortgage).

Free markets are a good thing, but they can be subject to excessive swings—both to the positive and the negative. As the pendulum swung to the excess, the negative consequences began to build behind the scenes.

In the 1990s, the subprime market began to mature through competition. New players were attracted to this previously untapped market as they recognized the opportunity and went for their piece of the pie. In any market system, as competition increases, so does the necessity to offer something different from all the rest. Mortgage lenders therefore created new products to keep the momentum going. The result was more aggressive lending standards:

- Lending to consumers with lower credit scores
- Lending a larger percentage of the value of the home
- Relaxed income documentation requirements, including less time on the job and other standards

In other words, subprime mortgages made sense for some buyers and some lenders in the beginning. But competition among lenders led to increasingly lax requirements, not only creating loan products that were bad for consumers, but also allowing some folks into the housing market who had no business being there. And what happened during the process is the crux of what led to the mortgage meltdown that began in the summer of 2007.

In order to allow for the more aggressive credit standards, Wall Street devised very creative structures to enable the sale of subprime mortgages to investors. These structures were formed through a process known as *securitization*, in which mortgages were pooled, then cut into pieces based on their value, and sold to investors in the form of bonds that were backed by the mortgages themselves. The bonds were rated to provide a measure of the inherent risk of each of the pieces; and in certain cases, the bonds were insured.

With the securitization process firmly in place, the subprime industry grew rapidly, and along with it increasingly relaxed credit standards as the structures used to sell the loans were adapted to the market. What started as a reasonable credit decision—lending to a borrower with a low credit score based upon that borrower's income and a home value far exceeding the amount of the loan—became more and more aggressive as a result of the ability of lenders to sell these loans into securitizations enabled by Wall Street.

As the market grew, it created a credit gap between subprime (borrowers with low credit scores) and A-grade (agency-quality loans with strong income and high credit scores) borrowers. The credit gap simply meant there were borrowers who fell in the middle who were being underserved—they could not qualify for an agency loan, but they had stronger financial positions than the typical subprime borrower. This credit gap was closed in the 1990s with the introduction of "Alternative A" loans (so named since the loans were not quite of A quality and not quite D—so give it a B-minus and a passing grade).

Now that the entire credit spectrum had been served and pretty much anyone with a pulse could obtain a loan, the mortgage markets experienced explosive growth.

Brewing Offshore

By the start of the new millennium, the perfect storm was brewing offshore. The bread and butter of the subprime industry was the "2/28" mortgage. This mortgage was fixed at a low rate for two years and adjustable for the remaining twenty-eight years, with rapidly increasing adjustments to the rate beginning in the third year—and with it, rapidly increasing payments. By the third year in one of these loans, most borrowers experienced payment shock and returned to refinance at a new two-year, introductory rate. This created borrower dependency on the ability to refinance once every several years and provided repeat business for mortgage originators. Both borrowers and industry alike became refinance addicts—the former by necessity and the latter by design.

> **Both borrowers and industry alike became refinance addicts—the former by necessity and the latter by design.**

The eventual inability of borrowers to consistently refinance their debt was the single most visible sign that big trouble was brewing in the housing market. The ability to refinance a mortgage is generally dependent upon the following:

1. The availability of credit
2. The ability to qualify for the credit
3. The existence of home equity

Because it could easily cost the borrower an average of $8,000 to refinance the typical subprime loan—and these costs were added to the new loan balance each time—home equity was slowly being stripped away, leaving less and less room to refinance. It follows that the ability to escape payment shock in the third year of a subprime loan relied on rising home values. This, in turn, made it clear that the entire subprime business, particularly in relation to high LTV lending practices, relied on increasing home prices in order to sustain itself. This fact alone should have provided plenty of warning that a serious storm was brewing on the horizon, but sometimes the weather looks really great just before things turn ugly.

Gaining Steam

The stage was set for the perfect storm in the housing and credit markets. The wide offering of credit seeded the dark clouds on the horizon, but a hurricane has to start spinning in order to gather some muscle. That spin came in the form of a declining interest rate cycle that began in 2001, making rates lower than they'd been in forty years. Low interest rates are generally favorable for housing prices, but once-in-a-lifetime interest-rate lows, combined with the following factors, made for an excessively overheated housing market:

Lending practices

Increasingly aggressive lending practices greatly widened the population of home buyers, both for primary residences and investment properties. The use of exotic mortgages and loose underwriting standards pushed housing demand to new levels never experienced before.

Short-term rates

Intermediate adjustable-rate mortgages, such as the 2/28 mortgage described earlier in this chapter, are typically fixed for two, three, five, seven, or ten years and then become adjustable. The shorter the fixed period, the lower the introductory rate. By far, the two-, three-, and five-year products were the most popular, mostly because of the discounts they offered from traditional thirty-year fixed-rate loans. Temporary purchasing power was thereby created for both a larger home and other purchases due to the low payments for the first two to five years. Many households refinanced, giving up good thirty-year fixed-rate loans at 5 percent to 6 percent for the attractiveness of rates as low as 3.5 percent. Households became accustomed to low payments and high levels of discretionary cash, not thinking ahead to the time when rates would return to normal levels.

Consumerism

Household spending increased dramatically as home owners tapped their equity through refinancing and home-equity loans. Consumers began to live as if the cost of debt wouldn't rise, raising their standard of living beyond their means and constantly depleting any cash reserves that would be needed when the inevitable market correction occurred.

Absence of regulation

Government exercised very little regulation over lending practices, despite the obvious warning signs of an overheated housing market. As a matter of fact, the Federal Reserve appeared to condone these practices at the time. Then-chairman Alan Greenspan made the following comments in a speech (you can read a transcription of the entire speech at www.federalreserve.gov/boarddocs/speeches/2004/20040223/) at the Credit Union National Association 2004 Government Affairs Conference in Washington, D.C., on February 23, 2004:

> Recent research within the Federal Reserve suggests that many home owners might have saved tens of thousands of dollars had they held adjustable-rate mortgages rather than fixed-rate mortgages during the past decade, though this would not have been the case, of course, had interest rates trended sharply upward . . . American consumers might benefit if lenders provided greater mortgage product alternatives to the traditional fixed-rate mortgage. To the degree that households are driven by fears of payment shocks but are willing to manage their own interest rate risks, the traditional fixed-rate mortgage may be an expensive method of financing a home.

You can replace the words *saved tens of thousands of dollars* in the above quote with *created tens of thousands of dollars of spendable cash.* That cash would undoubtedly have gone into the economy, not into the savings accounts of those home owners. Certainly the possible economic stimulus provided by this cash could have spurred the chairman's comments, however suspect that stimulus might be due to its temporary nature. In addition, the chairman made reference to the expensive nature of fixed-rate financing as opposed to the temporary savings offered by adjustable-rate mortgages, implying that consumers *willing* to manage interest-rate risk have the *ability* to manage interest-rate risk. We know all too well how that has panned out.

The makings of a very serious housing bubble were firmly in place at the time of the chairman's comments and it seems suspect that the Federal Reserve had no clue of the risks associated with the lending environment at the time. An unsustainable economy that depended on rising home values in order to support the high rate of consumer spending was firmly in place. The trigger would be an inevitable cycle of increasing rates, which would at the very least flatten home prices. Those who had leveraged their homes above 80 percent of value, particularly anyone with adjustable-rate mortgages, had put themselves at serious risk of the inability to refinance to a more affordable loan once the interest-rate cycle reversed itself.

Beginning in 2004, in order to curb inflationary pressures, the Federal Reserve began to slowly increase the federal funds rate (this is the rate at which banks borrow from the nation's central bank). This rate normally affects all other interest rates, including mortgages. From June 2004 to June 2006, the federal funds rate increased from 1 percent to 5.25 percent. For a period of time, long-term rates remained low relative to these increases to short-term rates, but this trend unraveled and by the beginning of 2005, long-term mortgage rates began to increase. With rising interest rates, a category-five financial hurricane was swelling offshore and preparing to hit the United States.

Slamming Ashore

The interest rate hikes in early 2006 had a delayed impact on the housing market. By the end of the year, increased rates took their toll on adjustable-rate mortgage borrowers, in particular the 2/28 subprime mortgages that were into the third year and beyond. These borrowers saw their payments rapidly increase, and mortgage delinquencies on a national level began to spike sharply. Home prices began to flatten, even deflate in some areas, in a natural response both to the monetary policy of increasing rates and in a sign the wild run-up in housing prices was ending. Borrowers with little or no equity in their homes realized that there was no room to refinance and were now stuck in payment shock. Investors in mortgage-backed securities reacted quickly to the situation and liquidity for new subprime mortgages began to dry up. By mid-2007, many subprime companies began to collapse, and the rest of the mortgage industry was close behind.

In the beginning, the crisis was referred to as the subprime mortgage crisis. In reality, it was an adjustable-rate mortgage crisis. If you think about it, what's the difference between a subprime mortgage that's fixed for two years and a prime mortgage that's fixed for three to five years? We know by now the answer is *not much*. Prime borrowers may have better credit scores, higher incomes, and live in better neighborhoods, but that's all relative to the amount of debt that's being carried. The prime market was just as ripe for a fall and investors realized this by the end of 2007. Fear began to grip the credit markets as investors become unwilling to buy mortgage-backed securities. As liquidity for new mortgages dried up, further declines in home prices followed, and delinquencies increased as more and more borrowers found they could not refinance their way out of their dilemma.

In the beginning, the crisis was referred to as the subprime mortgage crisis. In reality, it was an adjustable-rate mortgage crisis.

By 2008, the storm was in full swing and the full reality of the consequences of the excessive lending policies and the housing run-up of the early 2000s became apparent. Investment and savings banks began to fail in succession. Housing prices dropped by more than 50 percent in some areas and the Dow Jones Industrial Average plummeted by over 50 percent. Today, the housing market is in a tailspin. The mortgage troubles go far beyond subprime loans to the entire spectrum of mortgages, as leveraged consumers are faced with making mortgage payments they can't afford on a home that's worth less than the amount that they owe.

It Was Broken Before It Busted

The amazing thing about the credit crisis and the ensuing economic collapse is that we were in big trouble early on—but people feel safe when their home prices are increasing and the 401(k) balance is healthy, regardless of whether they have enough cash in the bank to weather a storm. Those leveraged households financed by adjustable-rate mortgages were naked against rising rates and therefore broke on paper, and broke on paper eventually leads to busted. If you study historical mortgage interest rates, you'll see that an average rate rests in the 7 to 8 percent range. Indeed, there were many times in the past forty years that 10 percent was a good mortgage rate. How many home owners with adjustable-rate mortgages took the time to pencil out how their finances would look if rates climbed to 8 percent?

The simple fact that rates were at lifetime lows should have been like a beacon shining on a rocky shoreline, warning you that your ship would crash into the rocks if you didn't take evasive action. That evasive action was to move from adjustable-rate loans to fixed-rate loans while housing values and interest rates supported this tactic.

INSIDER VIEWPOINT:
It Could Have Been Avoided

Can you imagine how much better off we'd be if people who had the ability to refinance out of adjustable mortgages before the crash had acted? Moreover, think about the damage that would have been avoided had adjustable-rate mortgages not been used in the first place. Predominant use of fixed-rate financing would have put a cap on housing prices as consumers were priced out of the market. Moreover, home owners would have had the protection and security of a constant payment and a more sustainable household economy. Certainly, the kind of widespread damage seen in the recession that took hold in 2008 would have been largely avoided.

Someone's Got to Pay

When you borrow money, someone's got to pay. If you stop making your payments, you'll lose what you purchased with the money you borrowed. In the case of a mortgage, that's your home. This usually isn't a problem for the bank or investor, since there's normally enough equity to pay off your loan and then some. But what happens when the value of the collateral that secures a loan is *less* than the *amount* of the loan? Lenders normally compensate for losses due to this problem by hiking the interest rate. The idea is the money received from people who pay covers the people who don't pay, so when you net it all out, there's an acceptable profit. That's why the rate on credit cards is so high—to compensate for losses because the credit granted is *unsecured*. You can't repossess a vacation!

Mortgages carry lower interest rates because the credit granted is secured; you *can* repossess a home. That's why it's so important to lend only a portion of the value of the home. Aggressive lending practices (such as 100 percent financing) were mitigated by rising real estate values; the earlier in the cycle a lender made a loan, the safer the loan appeared to be. But these practices are what continued to fuel housing, pushing prices up and creating a cycle of increasingly bold loan products in order to squeeze borrowers into homes they could only afford as long as rates remained low.

The mortgage industry—indeed, the entire financial system—wasn't designed to withstand the pressures we face today. One might expect a 20 percent or even a 30 percent correction in the market once a real estate bubble pops, but 50 percent or more? That's disaster.

A society that doesn't live within its means eventually has to pay the price. Certainly we have witnessed disaster and, one way or another, we're all going to pay for it. Delaying the pain with stimulus packages will only cause more pain down the road.

Loan Modification—The New Household Term

Once the mess was in full swing, society at large was well aware of the term *loan modification*. This isn't a refinance, it's an adjustment to the terms of your loan to create relief where there is no other alternative to the lender. Loan modifications become a necessity when borrowers default, there isn't home equity, and homes aren't selling. A foreclosure won't solve the problem. Like a mortgage, someone's got to pay for the loan modification. There are three problems with loan modifications that will cause all of us to feel the pain:

1. The cost

Mortgage servicers, the folks that collect your payment on behalf of investors or banks, normally earn from 0.25 percent to 0.5 percent as compensation for this duty. The economics of the mortgage business have been built on long-standing convention, and mortgage servicing is no exception. The system was not built to withstand the level of modifications brought on by the meltdown, hence mortgage loan servicers are stretched to deal with the influx. Since investors each have their own set of economics, the willingness to modify loans and pay more for this service varies. As a result, the government has stepped in to provide funds to mortgage servicers as an incentive to staff up, as well as offering compensation to investors to allow loan modifications (so long as the modification meets the government's standards).

2. Economics

Let's say you and I own a bank. We have some bad loans, but not as many as the next bank. Our financial circumstances dictate the terms of a loan modification, assuming we are willing to do one. In a free market, we have the right to make this determination, and because of the free market, the terms of a loan modification will vary from bank to bank and investor to investor. This causes confusion in the marketplace when the inevitable inconsistencies are discovered: one guy gets a break and the next guy loses his home. Now the guy who didn't get a break and is upside down decides it's better to just hand over the keys and walk away, leaving the bank with an asset it can't sell.

3. Entitlement

The third and worst problem is entitlement. There is widespread misunderstanding of the economics related to loan modification and, quite frankly, in a free-market system the lender who took the risk to make the loan should be able to determine who obtains a loan modification and who doesn't.

The actions taken by the government create further confusion as to who qualifies and who doesn't. Add to this the number of bailouts the government has spawned and you can see how a sense of entitlement can form in the mind of a home owner who is upside down on his mortgage.

Think about this as if you owned the bank and it was your money at stake. The bank has a business contract with the home owner. As business owners operating in the free market, we understand no one is entitled to a loan modification. It is purely our decision based upon the economics we face at any given time. However, as the sense of entitlement spreads, more and more of the loans we have on our books start to go delinquent, and all of a sudden the tail is wagging the dog.

But why should you (the bank owner) respond at all? When it comes down to it, no one twisted that borrower's arm to get into debt—remember, it was a business contract (even if the consumer was misguided). Nonetheless, to avoid committing the same mistakes all over again, as a society, we must stand and face the consequences.

No Free Lunch

It doesn't matter what rhetoric the government, media, or society feeds you. There is no free lunch and there are no bailouts. Someone's got to pay back every dollar that's been borrowed. All of it—every dime is going to come back out of our pockets one way or another. This takes many forms, including:

- As the government prints money to fund bailouts, prop up the mortgage market, and hold interest rates at artificially low levels, the risk of serious inflation grows significantly. Every American is going to pay in the form of higher prices for everything—including necessities such as food and clothing. Economist Milton Friedman once said, "Inflation is taxation without legislation." Don't be fooled into believing the government is doing a good thing by printing money day and night to help us out.
- Reduction on the value of your home and your investments.
- Increased taxes on individuals and businesses, which in turn further inflate prices.
- Higher costs of energy to operate your home and fuel to operate your vehicles.
- Lost jobs as companies feel the pinch and cut back during the tough times and slow job growth as employers stretch to do more with less as the economy slowly recovers.

What led to the credit crisis in the first place is financially irresponsible living. Let's not blame the system—we're the ones who should have said no and saved for a rainy day. I'm sure there are many who did the right things and have felt the pain of the economic

> *It doesn't matter what rhetoric the government, media, or society feeds you. There is no free lunch and there are no bailouts. Someone's got to pay.*

meltdown, even though they didn't deserve it. But a financially broken society can also break those who are fiscally responsible. Life's not generally about what one deserves—yet it is about what we can learn from it.

The lesson is to accept responsibility, take action, and adjust our way of life. Handing forth a bailout is like giving a former alcoholic a shot of whiskey. He forgets everything he learned from the recovery process and starts drinking again. Like the alcoholic, there are permanent societal changes required. Revisions in our buying and spending behavior must be implemented if our nation is to recover soundly from the credit crisis.

Governments don't learn—people do. The government can't do it for you. You must take action. You must get right with your finances.

INSIDER VIEWPOINT:
It's Going to Happen Again

I received the nice-looking postcard in my mailbox soliciting a refinance. As I read the print, my stomach started to turn. The headline read "Savings Starts with Your Home" and the pitch went like this:

Want to own your home faster and save money along the way? If you enjoy great value, this mortgage is for you:

- *5-year fixed loan at 3.99 percent (4.06 percent APR)*
- *Same low rate for loans up to $750,000*
- *Free biweekly payments so you can own your home sooner*
- *Set it and forget it with automatic and electronic payments*
- *Low closing costs*

The following table summarized the salient points, assuming a $250,000 mortgage:

Loan	% of Home Value Borrowed	Rate	APR	Biweekly Payment	Payment Period
Easy Mortgage	75% or less	3.99%	4.06%	$619.89	Year 1–5

Final payment: $228,718.06

What's wrong with this picture? Gee—where should we start?

* The rate is only good for five years; what happens after that?
* There isn't any value in "free" biweekly payments. You can achieve the same result by simply adding to your monthly payment. It's an empty promise and it's all spin.
* The biweekly payment looks nice—it's a great way for

the lender to make the payment look very appealing—
but that's not the true monthly cost for the loan.

This mortgage solicitation is focused on the payment—something we'll discuss further in detail. But there is something much more disturbing than any of the subtle problems listed above. Look at the words *Final payment: $228,718.06*. This mortgage is a five-year *balloon* mortgage. That means it's payable in full at the end of five years—and if you don't qualify for a refinance at that time, you'll lose your house if you can't make that huge payment. Nice easy mortgage: easy for the lender to foreclose five years down the road. (Notice the percent of home value borrowed is 75 percent or less.)

It's a fairly safe bet to assume rates will climb within the next five years (which is precisely why the bank is offering the loan—it's forced to be paid off so they can invest their money at better rates down the road). Given thirty-year mortgage rates were at fifty-year lows when I received this mailer, you should be in shock that a lender would suggest this is a good deal. Absolutely in shock!

Didn't we just learn loans such as these are what got us into trouble in the first place? Did we learn *anything* from the credit crisis? Anyone who falls for this ridiculous pitch is setting himself up for the sequel to the credit crisis.

5

GET RIGHT
WITH YOUR FINANCES

Trent and Lisa: The Mole Game

There's a game Trent and Lisa's four-year-old son loves to play. You stick a couple of quarters in the slot, pick up a rubber mallet, and whack the moles as they pop their heads up out of the holes. Every time you whack one down, another pops up. Whack it down and yet another one appears. And then another.

After Trent and Lisa pay their bills, they usually spend the rest and barely make it to the next paycheck. With the mortgage, two cars, the credit card payments, and a student loan, there's not much left after they pay their bills, but some months are better than others. They try to save, but there's always something that seems to blow the month.

Trent and Lisa didn't plan their finances along the way—buying a home, acquiring the cars, and buying some nice things on credit. They looked at the payments and figured they'd be able to make them.

But the moles keep popping up. Month after month after month. They just can't seem to get ahead.

The savings rate in the United States prior to the economic meltdown of 2008 was less than 1 percent. Consumer spending normally accounts for 70 percent of the economy. I've long believed that the moment American citizens began to live financially responsible lives, the economy would tank. The rate of consumer spending we became accustomed to simply isn't sustainable. Permanent adjustments must be made, and that starts with us. It is not patriotic to jump back in and spend like there's no tomorrow—we must only buy what we need and be wise about buying what we think we need. The good news is that once the economy adjusts, if consumers remain responsible, the country will be better off for it.

In order to stay on a course that won't find you wrecked on shore, you need to get right with your finances. The bottom line is that you must live within your means. This isn't a new concept, but all of us have blown it at one time or another. There isn't an alternative here—it's something you need to understand and adhere to.

If you want to know what's important to someone, take a look at his calendar and his checkbook.

Getting right with your finances is a matter of perspective and discipline. It's a process that starts with getting out from under your debt (and the related stress) and discovering a lifestyle that is more rewarding, regardless of how appealing the lifestyle being sold by the culture may be (it's the lifestyle sold by the culture that got you into debt in the first place).

Here's a simple exercise you'll find revealing. If you want to know what's important to someone, take a look at his calendar and his checkbook. Try this on yourself for size. What kinds of activities are reflected in your calendar, and where is your money going? Do they reflect the lifestyle you desire—or do they reflect something much different?

Behavioral and Situational Spending

Behavioral spending has to do with your attitudes and what's important to you. Behavioral spending that is based on impulse and the "desire to acquire" will lead to big trouble. Not that acquiring certain things that are important to you is bad, but it's toxic if it leads to upside-down finances.

Behavioral spending is often driven by your emotional quotient, which is driven by outside influences. Those influences begin with our culture of consumerism and, if you aren't careful, it's really easy to get wrapped up in it.

I live in south Orange County in Southern California. It's almost too perfect. The weather is fabulous, and there are a lot of great neighborhoods with nicely appointed homes that have professionally manicured landscapes and backyards with pools. Nearly every home has at least two nice cars parked in the garage (if not another on the driveway) and at least a few toys alongside—a boat, Jet Skis, motorcycles, you name it. Everyone has a gardener and a housekeeper and many have nannies to watch the kids while mom and dad go to work. Most kids are provided with all the "necessary" gadgets and electronics, and by the time they can drive they are given a car. Trouble is, I don't see many kids working in the local stores, but I see them in the malls shopping to their hearts' content.

What you see in my local neighborhood is a result of behavioral spending driven by culture. It's a reflection of what's important to people—and it feeds on itself, because as you view it, it distorts and pulls you in to do the same. And it pollutes the next generation with a sense of entitlement to a lifestyle that the previous generation ignorantly allowed. It doesn't take a rocket scientist to imagine that very few of the households where I live have six months of cash in the bank, are socking away at least 10 percent into their retirement accounts, and have a solid college savings plan for their kids. But they bought them each a car! It's a safe bet that these households are overloaded with debt and are just a few months or less from bankruptcy should something go wrong.

Behavioral spending, as it pertains to material items, is usually associated with the payment. The question is always *What do I qualify for?* rather than *How much can I afford?* Just because you can afford the payment doesn't mean you can afford to own that new car or put a pool in the backyard. You must think of everything that goes with it. Insurance costs go up after buying that sports car (and even higher should you get a traffic ticket). The expensive tires need to be replaced. The pool in your backyard needs service because the pump went out. You don't have time to clean the pool because you are too busy working to make the payments, so you hire a pool service to do it for you.

The payments generated by behavioral spending give rise to the inability to deal with situational expenses. Situations give rise to surprise expenses every month. You can count on it. The air conditioning goes out on the hottest day of the year. You have a tire blow out. The pipes in the kitchen burst. One of your kids gets sick. You get sick. The brakes on your car need to be replaced. You find a leak in your roof during a rainstorm. Shall I go on?

Behavior must become the first objective in managing your money. And this behavior starts with one main perspective: *if you don't have the cash, you don't buy it.*

The Role of Debt

Jeremy and Tricia: Smacked by the Swine

The piggy bank just sits on the shelf, more a decoration than anything else. Jeremy and Tricia have all the toys, their kids lacking nothing.

The mortgage payment made it easy to buy what they wanted. The rate on the new loan was only 3.99 percent and it was good for five years. With a payment of only $1,625, there was room to upgrade one of the cars, adding another $300 per month. With a lot more room to borrow (at least from the bank's perspective), the great credit card offers came rolling in. Before they knew it, they owed $10,000. A mortgage refinance took care of that; along with some cash out and a great rate of 4.25 percent for another five years, their payment was only $1,900.

But then the credit card cycle kicked in once again. By the time they had $15,000 racked up, some new offers came in to transfer their credit card debt from one bank to another—with interest at 5 percent for the first three months—right through the end of summer. Another $7,000 was tacked on after a trip to Hawaii, a getaway to the Bahamas, and back-to-school shopping.

The payments and the cost of upkeep for everything they had acquired crept up on them. It became more difficult to make ends meet, and the credit card balance started to grow each month to fund the shortfall. Before they knew it, they owed $30,000 in credit card debt and had maxed out all that could be borrowed against their home.

Then Tricia lost her job and Jeremy's bonuses got cut. Now they're fighting for a mortgage loan modification and have signed up for credit counseling.

No retirement savings. No college savings. But the kids have nice clothes and the latest video games in the entertainment room—right where the swine sits on the shelf. He's a bit dusty, but if he could get up, he'd shake it off and smack a few folks around for being forced to sit there and watch everyone party while he starved to death.

Debt can sneak up on you and trap you in a never-ending stream of payments. The word *payment* is the key to understanding how to use debt wisely. The problem most consumers face is that they go for the bait of the easy monthly payment the credit industry uses to lure them into spending any extra money they may have. Virtually everything can be bought on a payment plan, thereby making it affordable to purchase something that you don't have the cash to buy. Now, it's reasonable to purchase a home or a new car on a payment plan, but it's another thing entirely to take on the burden of a larger mortgage or car loan than you can afford, or to extend this buying behavior into other areas and pile up loans on things you don't have the cash to buy, simply because you want them now. You know you've overused credit when you find yourself carrying balances on several credit cards and payments on loans other than your home and the automobiles you use for transportation. Worse yet, you know you are living far beyond your means when the credit card balances increase each month.

I believe the problem begins in our culture. Material possessions are inaccurately associated with financial success and freedom. This cultural definition of success is fueled by readily available credit, giving virtually anyone with a job and decent credit the ability to make purchases that go far beyond his means. Advertising agencies are extremely adept at stimulating your desire for that shiny new car, a luxury vacation, or a new boat, and the credit industry is right behind them just waiting to cut you a check in return for years of monthly payments. The payments soon begin piling on, as those in the credit industry that don't yet have a piece of your pie solicit any additional capacity you have to borrow.

> *Material possessions are inaccurately associated with financial success and freedom.*

Ironically, it actually becomes easier to acquire more credit once you've built a payment stream, allowing you to further consume and slowly become a slave to your possessions. Very soon, what you once viewed as success becomes drudgery. Your payments continue long after the luster of the new car or that larger home has worn off—and all of a sudden, you feel trapped by a mountain of monthly bills and loan payments.

Pretty much everyone has experienced some form of what I've described above. Ask anyone if they would gladly give up the payments they've accumulated and trade in the assets acquired for more time with their family, more freedom to change jobs if they so desire, and less stress when the monthly payments come around.

That feeling of entrapment is a direct result of buying things on payment. It is the single worst enemy to a healthy financial situation for the American family.

So what is a person to do about this problem? The answer is to come up with a plan to correct the situation. That plan is simple: stop acquiring and focus on getting out of debt. This is easier said than done and will normally take a fairly long time, but once you are on the right path, you'll find yourself desiring fewer material things and you'll enjoy the resulting freedom so much that you won't go back!

To start this process, you need to understand the proper role debt plays in your overall financial picture. There are only four reasons to borrow money:

1. Adequate housing
2. Adequate transportation
3. To pay for college
4. A medical emergency

That's it—except for rare occasions, debt must be limited to your house and your car! This goes against what the vast majority of your friends and neighbors are doing, but understanding it is imperative to gaining control over your finances. Let me illustrate by using your home as an example of the right and wrong ways of managing debt.

Let's say you purchase a home that would be adequate for you and your family for many years to come (notice the use of the word *adequate*). You purchase this home using a plain vanilla thirty-year fixed-rate loan and you avoid any superfluous uses of debt. Over time, you'll notice the following key benefits:

- As your income increases, your payment becomes more and more affordable because it's fixed (it's inflation proof).
- You generate increasing discretionary cash, which you can use to save for a rainy day, pay off your home faster, invest in your retirement, or invest in your children's education.
- You accumulate increasing home equity, which can later be used to supplement your retirement, if need be.

These benefits are the signs of a healthy, sustainable household economy. They are in stark contrast to the typical situation that evolves for many home owners:

- As your income increases, you experience increased borrowing capacity and you use this capacity to acquire nicer cars, to redecorate the home, and a variety of other things.
- Your house payments increase over time as you refinance to tap home equity in order to make home improvements and purchase big-ticket items.
- You refinance to consolidate your car and credit card payments, further extending your mortgage well into your retirement years.
- You are left with little or no home equity, you have no savings that will help you weather a storm, you have no savings for retirement, and you are stretching to send your children to college (if at all).

As you can see, there is a markedly different lifestyle in these two households. Our culture would lead you to believe you should look ahead to owning a larger home as your income goes up and tap increasing home equity to fund your lifestyle. Clearly, however, the current economic circumstances in the United States confirm this is actually a path to disaster. What percentage of households would you venture to guess operate on an economically sustainable basis? Just taking a look around should give you a clue that it's a small minority.

Consumer Debt = No Money

What about other debts? It's important to distinguish among these other debts, which I'll refer to as consumer debt. These include credit cards, personal loans, and other means of financing household purchases, such as furnishings, electronics, and so forth. As to all these other debts, you need to understand the following concept and how it affects your finances:

If you have any consumer debt and you have less cash than is needed to offset the cost of the debt, you have no money.

What does this mean? Consider this example: you have $10,000 of credit card debt at 18 percent, which costs you $1,800 per year or $150 per month to carry. In order for you to break even on the cost of carrying this debt by generating interest income of $1,800, you would need to have savings of $45,000 at 4 percent! That's more than four times the amount of your debt. If you look at it this way, it's easy to conclude that most people effectively have no money after netting out the cost of their debt.

In this example, everything you purchase with your disposable income is being financed at 18 percent. That's because if you have an extra $500 and you spend it—rather than paying down your debt—interest continues to pile up on the unpaid balance. Think of it this way: it's not that you are paying interest on the things you bought with the credit card, you are paying interest on the money you are spending. You are paying the credit card company 18 percent for the privilege of spending your own money! The very thought of this should make you sick. Does it bother you to pay $3 to withdraw your money at an ATM? If the answer is yes, it should bother you just as much to pay interest on your credit cards for the right to spend your own money.

Consumer debt has nothing to do with what you've purchased; it represents a current and future claim on your money. You've heard the phrase "time is money." Well, in this instance, money is time—*your time.* You trade your time for the money you earn, and if the money you earn is constantly threatened by the existence of debt, it's just not a good trade.

> *Consumer debt has nothing to do with what you've purchased; it represents a current and future claim on your money.*

It is imperative that you understand this concept if you are going to become an expert at managing your finances and your mortgage. Mortgage debt, like all other debt, represents a claim on your money and time. Because of the long-term nature of mortgage debt, the cost of your spending and the resulting impact on your finances are far greater than you might think. This is why you need to understand the basics of how to prioritize your spending, which will help you pay down your debt and avoid new ones.

Spending Priorities

It's easy to come up with spending priorities if you take the time to think about it. The hard part is sticking to those priorities. You have to muster the motivation if you want to be successful in your financial life.

Although I haven't always done so, I strive to live on what I call the "Give, Save, and Live" plan:

- Give 10 percent
- Save 10 percent
- Live on 80 percent of what you make

There are many reasons to give at least 10 percent before you move on to saving and spending. What I have actually isn't mine; rather, it's on loan to me for as long as I am allowed to dwell on this earth. I came into this world without possessions, and I'll leave behind what I acquired when I depart. Giving off the top represents that my heart isn't attached to my money and to things I can't take with me when I go. It breaks me of materialism and it makes me think of those who are less fortunate than I am before I think of myself. As a Christian, it helps me to focus on God and the only eternal, physical beings on this earth: people. You can choose to accept or reject this contention. Regardless, giving should not come last on the list of how you steward your income. It has its rightful place, at the very least, before you spend money on luxuries and such.

Saving 10 percent off the top says that I'm more concerned about my family's future well-being than the here and now. It helps me insulate my family from the many storms that are sure to come along the road of life, and it better secures plans for later years when I might not want to work as hard as I did when I was young. Saving 10 percent of your income is actually *critical* to your overall financial picture—and 10 percent is the absolute *minimum*. If you've read any book on finances before this one, you know this rule. It's a stalwart principle of personal finance and an absolute must if you are going to break away from the all-too-common situation of reaching retirement age with little or no savings.

Included in your savings are your cash reserves. This might rock your world, but you need at least six months of cash reserves in order to have an adequate safety valve. It's doable, but only if you stay away from credit and live within your means. Emergencies and unforeseen circumstances will always arise. If you establish an emergency fund, you must replenish it after each time you tap into it. Managing your emergency fund is an eye-opening experience—you don't realize how much you have to set aside until you start tracking all the financial surprises in your life.

> *You need at least six months of cash reserves in order to have an adequate safety valve. It's doable, but only if you stay away from credit and live within your means.*

After giving and saving, you'll have 80 percent left to spend as needed, which includes paying your income taxes. In the interest of keeping things simple, your spending should fit within no more than ten categories, not counting emergencies and significant unforeseen circumstances (which should be funded by cash reserves accumulated from your savings plan). Here's the list:

1. Your home (your mortgage, property taxes, insurance, utilities, and other necessary expenses)
2. Groceries
3. Adequate clothing
4. Adequate transportation and related expenses
5. Paying down mortgage debt

6. Family and relationship-building activities (anything that uses money as a conduit to fostering relationships)
7. Education
8. Leisure activities and hobbies
9. "Nice to haves" (an extra cell phone, MP3 player, and so on)
10. Luxury items (big-ticket items such as a boat, a fancy sports car, or flashy clothes and jewelry)

Take a hard look at this simple list and then compare it to how you currently spend your money. If you have anything out of order, chances are your spending is way out of whack. Study your checkbook and you'll quickly see where you might have some problems.

Just less than half of the list pertains to necessities. I'll bet if you looked at the spending habits of most Americans, their list wouldn't be this short nor would at least half of it be associated with necessities. All of the necessities on the list—a home, transportation, and the like—are assumed to be of modest means and within your income. On many people's lists, leisure activities and luxury items—the "wants"—are on the top, and giving and saving are at the bottom.

Notice where paying down your mortgage debt appears on the list. The list assumes that you have no consumer or credit card debt. If this isn't the case, paying down consumer debts takes at least the same level of priority as savings does. As a matter of fact, paying off those debts must come before you consider savings goals that go beyond establishing an emergency cash fund.

If you spend within the priority ordered by this list, you'll actually find that you have more time for family and relationship-building activities. It's much better to have the money to do these things than to be strapped with another payment for the latest

Get Right with Your Finances

LCD television or some fancy entertainment system. Anything that is nice to have or is in the luxury category should come long after you've made the proper investment in your family, other relationships, and those in need. Try this, and I bet you'll find those things much more rewarding than almost anything else on the discretionary list.

Slavery

Debt is a form of slavery.

Once you have acquired debt, you are enslaved to the lender until you pay it off. If you've limited the use of debt to adequate housing and transportation, your payments will not be overly burdensome and it will feel far from slavery; at the most, an obligation to perform. If, on the other hand, you abuse debt by leveraging yourself, you'll find repayment to be a drudgery that lasts long after the initial excitement over your purchases has faded. You will become enslaved and your lifestyle will be affected because the majority of your income-producing efforts will be dedicated to paying off your debts. You will have to maintain a certain level of income in order to meet your obligations, which will limit your career choices and cause you grief during economic downtimes. In extreme cases, you'll be running from your creditors, who will seek you mercilessly until you have satisfied your obligations.

Debt forces you to trade your money for quality time and relationships. As you acquire and consume by piling on the debt, the quality of the time you have (there are only twenty-four hours to each day) and your relationships deteriorate as the stress level in your life increases. If you have experienced the kind of life that comes with a mountain of debt, you know what I'm talking about. It robs you of time by shifting the amount you are given each day to worrying about how you'll get out of the mess you are in. It places great strain on your marriage and reduces the flexibility you have in your schedule to invest in your children. It chains you to your job and a certain level of income, which becomes all the more burdensome should you wish to change jobs to something more emotionally rewarding (but which may pay less).

> *Getting into debt puts a current and future claim on you, your money, and your time that almost always causes more pain than any pleasure the possessions acquired have provided.*

I'll say it again: getting into debt puts a current and future claim on you, your money, and your time that almost always causes more pain than any pleasure the possessions acquired have provided.

Once you get out of debt, you'll most likely never go back. This is because it was easy to pile it on, but extremely painful to get rid of it. You'll find it makes you ill to think about paying interest, and the only reason you'll use a credit card is to rack up airline miles—but you'll pay off the balance every month. Because it was easy to get into debt and so much work to eliminate it, you'll appreciate the money you earn and become a wise steward of it. If you find you want some new toy, you'll pay cash for it and you'll think long and hard about your spending priorities and the impact on other members of your family before buying it. If that new toy challenges greater priorities, you'll find it better to stay away from it.

This kind of thinking doesn't exist for the person who is just a card swipe away from acquiring their latest desires.

INSIDER TIP:

Think of Your Home as a Business

If you think of running your personal finances as a business, you'll create a viable, secure situation for your family.

A business must make profits to survive. This means the business must make a return on the assets it employs, such as people to run the business, a factory to manufacture products, and a delivery system to bring products to consumers. If the business borrows money, it must be used to improve profits in order to justify taking out a loan. If there are no profits—if the business takes in less than it earns—it will go broke.

Your home is the same in many ways. Your savings are your profits, and if you don't have any, you will not survive. This means you must earn a return on the major assets you employ: your home accumulates equity over time, your car derives income because it provides transportation to and from work, and you make investments that provide a return on your savings. If you borrow money, it must improve your savings (profits). Thus you use a mortgage to buy only the home you can afford, you don't tap equity in order to buy depreciating assets, and you *never* use credit cards.

You create an environment for your children that will set them up to be productive members of society—you want them to become people who are resources, not people who use resources. You can't do that if your financial life doesn't foster savings and serves as a poor example.

Unlike a business, you operate your home with the vision of *going out of business*. Your kids will be on their own someday, and you will be engaged only for as long as you continue to work. You must have a source of income planned after you close up shop. The revenue in your post-work era is your retirement savings—and if you don't get right with your finances, you'd better plan to be in business for a really long time.

Living Free
Matthew: Who Wants to Be a Millionaire?

Matthew is fresh out of college and has just entered the workforce. He had a finance professor who was adamant that almost every American could retire a millionaire. When Matthew first heard this, he didn't buy it. So many people don't have a lot of money—how could it be?

But then the professor showed the class what the power of time and math can do. If you save $200 per month in your 401(k) the moment you take that first job, with a 10 percent return, you'll have saved $1,275,000 after forty years (without an employer match)! Surely anyone can set aside $200 per month. His finance professor demonstrated how most households had more than $200 per month in payments in addition to their mortgages and automobiles.

Then things got really interesting. What if you took $200 a month and increased the amount you set aside monthly by $50 each year? Certainly that's doable. The results were astounding—in the neighborhood of $4 million!

If he sticks to his guns, Matthew can accomplish all of this wealth building by taking what's necessary right off the top of his paycheck. Great results, considering the fact that this occurs before engaging in an aggressive plan to pay down any mortgage debt he might acquire.

Matthew is determined not to sign up for a house he can't afford and fancy things that rack up credit card bills. He's witnessed the pain caused by the economic crisis and he's got time on his side. He has other things on his mind. He wants to live free of the burdens of debt. He's part of a new generation and his life is going to be different. Much, much different.

Think about the Give, Save, and Live approach to your finances. Your interpretation of the phrase depends upon how you read it. It means you live *as a result* of having given and saved first. And this leads to a *life* of freedom.

How so?

It circles back to your priorities and how they reflect the intent of your life.

Let's go back to your checkbook and your calendar. Take a good, hard look at the entries and ask yourself, *Is my life intentional or accidental?* and *If it's intentional, what's the intent?* It's pretty easy to tell by examining how you spend your time and your money.

Life can be intentional or it can simply be accidental. The intentional life is either about you or about others:

- When it's about you, you'll be concerned about making an impression:

    What do others think of me? How do I look? What can I do to impress them? Are my kids only good at sports or are they also good with people?

- When it's about others, you'll be concerned about making an impact:

  What can I do to help my spouse? What can I do to help my children grow up to be responsible adults? How can I use what I have to make the world a better place? How can I serve the needs of others?

Your finances follow the intent of your life. An intentional financial life reflects how you are living and what you are living for: it's either all about you or it's about others.

How many of us actually spend the time to ponder how we are living? Perhaps most of us have some idea of what we are living for. If you do, then there's a good chance it will define how you are living. For example, if a person lives to obtain material wealth, then how that person lives is dedicated to this cause. But it's not that simple. There are a number of things that people live for simultaneously. The most obvious are things such as providing for a family, obtaining career status, and saving for retirement. Try this: make a list of what you are living for and put them into one of two categories:

1. Wealth and success: advancement of your career for the sake of status, money, or power; and tangible objects such as a car, house, or boat.
2. Significance and people: focusing on matters of significance, dedication to your faith, and acting in a manner that reflects your faith; taking the time to become more intimate with your spouse, being available to your children and your family, and building meaningful relationships; coaching, mentoring, and encouraging others in your workplace; and caring for other people.

As you compile the list, be honest about it. If you keep a calendar, examine the entries for the past six months. Review each entry in your checkbook for the last six months as well. Relate the entries in both to the list.

Now step back and look at the list. How many of the entries in your calendar and checkbook fall into the wealth and success category, and how many fall into the significance and people category? I'm not talking about the amount of time you spend—full-time employment takes up the majority of your waking hours—I'm talking about how you use the time you have. What is the intent of the activities while you are at work? Are they primarily aimed at wealth and success or matters of significance and people? In your spare time for the people category, are there any activities serving the needs of people who are outside your immediate family and circle of friends?

What does your spending reflect? Which category takes precedence? If it's the first, that's why your finances are a mess.

It follows that *what* you are living for defines *how* you are living. Those who are concerned first with wealth and success as defined by the culture will live their lives seeking money, possessions, power, and pleasure. They will seek to please themselves and impress others as a way to affirm their existence as meaningful. They love money and as a result use people to get it. Those who are concerned first with significance and people live their lives seeking to employ their time in a manner that reflects their faith and values. They define success within the context of significance, placing people above all else—people in their families, the workplace, and the community. They see wealth as a by-product of success, not as the primary motivating factor *for* success.

There is yet another way of living. While intentional living has a purpose (whether centered on self or centered on others), accidental living is living without a purpose and with no mission in mind. In this manner of living, a person consumes resources for his own benefit and seeks temporary pleasures to offset the routine or mundane circumstances of life. His finances reflect this type of living, as money is merely a means to a temporary and impulsive end.

Many people live accidentally. They swing along with popular culture, which leads to inconsistency. There's no overall plan that is built on a foundation for living. As a result, these people fall into careers that they aren't happy with, enter marriages that they complain about, and have responsibilities they'd rather be without. Their relationships aren't deep and meaningful, being played out on the surface by way of superficial discussion and activities; they never achieve a level of human intimacy in which their spouse, other family members, and close friends truly know what makes them tick. As a consequence, they live lonely, self-centered lives (that they don't admit to), attempting to find satisfaction without ever truly investigating the meaning of their lives.

Our culture sells the intentional, self-centered and sometimes accidental life. Take a close look around and be honest about it—don't you see it? Advertisers know that people are generally dissatisfied with something in their lives. That's why they constantly pull on the strings of discontentment, selling you the latest fix to repair what is wrong or gain the affirmation or clout you are looking for. They position their products in such a way you end up comparing where you are to where you could be, how much you have to how much you could have, and how you look to how good you could look. And people chase the dream, only to find more discontentment, another payment to make, and the desire for another fix for the latest craving.

Living accidentally and living intentionally for oneself always lead to financial disaster and despair. Should you obtain the finances to do as you please, it will not, in itself, lead to happiness and contentment. Why is it that so many famous, very wealthy people end up miserable, despite acquiring all the world covets and society deems as worthy? A great example of this was Ernest Hemingway, who was revered as a man who had it all. In fact, *Playboy* magazine wrote an article that concluded that while the Bible claimed the wages of sin was death, the wages of sin sure paid off for Mr. Hemingway. Shortly thereafter, suffering from depression and distraught over what he saw as a meaningless life, he committed suicide.

If you want to be free, both financially and personally, don't live according to the pattern of the culture. Live an intentional life, with a noble cause for each component and a foundation upon which all the components come together with an end in mind.

As a Christian, I aim to lead an intentional life that is built on the conviction of my faith (instead of the swing of culture and popular opinion), with a focus on relationships instead of possessions, with the possessions I have being used as an avenue to relationships. There is an end in mind, which is actually a beginning—eternity. The end keeps me from craving the latest and greatest, since I know life itself is temporary and the latest and greatest certainly will fade much faster. This doesn't mean I don't like certain things. I have a 1955 Chevrolet (it's gorgeous), but it's not at the top of my list. What's great about the car is that it always generates a conversation that gives me the opportunity to get to know someone new. And it's a lot of fun to work on with my son. The car drives relationships (pun intended!).

Take a good, hard look at the intent of your life and how it ties to your finances. Everything you buy is going to go out of fashion, fade away, rust, or end up in the junk heap. Technology is moving so fast, you will most certainly go broke if you believe you must keep up with it. Everything—including your money—is temporary. The thrill of a new possession is no match for the smile of your children, the affection of your spouse, having dinner listening to a friend in need, visiting with your neighbor, and so many other activities that involve people. You need time if you are going to enjoy these things—time that is only available to you if you aren't enslaved to your debts.

Focusing on the right things will protect your family from the credit industry's attempt to pilfer your home equity to fund what the culture is attempting to sell you. Once you break free from debt and the cultural definition of wealth and success, you'll find that you are living your own definition of wealth and success—and it's much more satisfying.

Money Isn't a Bad Thing

Don't get the wrong message from this chapter—money and a successful career are not bad things. Wanting these things is natural. But true wealth and success comes from the realization that wealth isn't what you spend—it's what you save. Once you've saved and attained wealth, you'll pay cash for the nicer things in life.

Money is important, as it allows you to spend time as you wish; a successful career is a rewarding and fulfilling experience. However, money and a great career are more rewarding and of much greater significance when they are the result of your focus on people as your first priority.

INSIDER VIEWPOINT:
They Are Counting on You

They are counting on you. Counting on you to leverage yourself all over again. Counting on you to mortgage your future just like the government has, so the economy can get buzzing again.

In contrast, it seems to me we've been forced to live more financially responsible lives. That's a good thing, despite how painful it might be along the way. It doesn't help to blame big business because they lent money to anyone who could fog a mirror. Neither is it going to help to have our government step in with bailout money to give the recovering credit alcoholics another shot of whiskey.

Going back to the culture of consumption that existed before we hit the skids isn't going to resolve anything in the long run. It's just going to defer the pain to another day. Our economy has been dependent on consumer spending at levels that aren't sustainable. Obviously, we're not seeing the level of spending we're used to. And we're all suffering from it. Could it be that this suffering is necessary to bring us back to reality? Could it be that the economy would be better off if consumer spending, as a percentage of household earnings, were to be permanently adjusted downward?

How much of consumer spending prior to the crash do you think was fueled by the use of credit? Credit cards. Home equity loans. Cash-out mortgage refinances. You name it, we used it. And now we're paying for it—either directly or indirectly.

Jobs and real earnings must fuel consumer spending—only after we have saved at the household level. If we don't learn this lesson, we will cease to prosper as a nation.

So here we are with nice, low interest rates once again. Just like before the great crash of 2008. These rates are supposed to entice lending, which in turn fuels spending. Do you want to participate by drinking the Kool-Aid, or do you want to recover from your bad habits once and for all?

They—the government—need you to go back out and spend. If you don't, we can't support the size the government has grown to. The tax base will shrink if we become savers. So the government will have to print money to stay in business, or increase taxes. Why do you think there is very little incentive built into the tax code to motivate you to save?

I say don't participate. They are counting on you to leverage yourself all over again by mortgaging your future away. Don't do it!

6

GET A GRIP ON MORTGAGE TROUBLE

Bill and Susan:
What Was Once Home Equity Is Now Nothing

Bill and Susan bought their house years ago, well before the great housing meltdown. They never really thought much about their mortgage debt, except for making sure they paid on time. Bill and Susan like to keep their finances straight—they save what they can each month and try to make good decisions.

Over the years, their home more than doubled in value. Both Bill and Susan worked and, together, they made a good living. It was easy to qualify for their refinance and they were able to obtain $130,000 in cash from the equity—now they could do some things they never dreamed possible. They took extra time off to enjoy a lavish vacation and used the rest of the money to install a swimming pool and tropical landscaping, transforming their backyard into a year-round vacation spot.

Interest rates were low, so the mortgage payments were low too; they never gave it another thought. They had the extra cash to buy new things for the house and furniture for their backyard oasis. With some money in the bank and equity in their home, they felt secure.

One day, they received a notice their payment was going up. They knew the loan was adjustable, but they were still surprised. It was a little harder to make the payments, but not all that bad. Six months later, it happened again and a few months after that, Susan lost her job. Now they were scrambling to make the payments, and while Bill was able to hold onto his job, his company slashed bonuses. The home they enjoyed and could once afford became a noose around their necks.

Had they left well enough alone, they would still have been able to afford the payments (and, of course, owe $130,000 less). Besides, Bill and Susan love the beach and find themselves taking a drive to walk along the shore more often than lazing around the pool.

They crossed the line into mortgage trouble the moment they received that big check. The recession had nothing to do with the fundamental problem—it just exacerbated it.

If only they could turn back the clock . . .

There are a number of paths that lead to mortgage trouble. Some of these are obvious and some of them are subtle with the trouble brewing over a period of time. Yet others occur by way of the very design of the mortgage industry. Let's look at the ways you can avoid trouble.

Buy on Price—Never on Payment!

Decisions based on the payment are the single largest contributors to mortgage trouble. In order to avoid problems, you must understand price so that you have a grasp on the total cost of acquiring new mortgage debt. You'll learn more about this in chapter 12.

The mortgage industry positions its products in a way that narrows your focus down to the payment. This benefits the mortgage company and misdirects your attention from more important things, like the total cost associated with your loan and other details that can cost you dearly down the road. Some of the dangers of this narrowed focus include:

- While the impact on the monthly payment of paying $1,000 more in fees than you have to seems small (it's spread over thirty years), if you paid $1,000 too much, you're still out $1,000 of cold, hard cash. In addition, unless you pay it down, you'll carry the overpayment, plus interest, for the life of the loan and all subsequent refinances. Overcharges can cost four to six times the original amount in the long run.
- When you refinance, you extend your payoff date by entering into a new thirty-year loan. For example, if you are in year five of a thirty-year loan, you'll add five years to your debt by refinancing. Adding those five years makes it easy for the new mortgage company to lower your payment and divert your attention from the total cost of the new debt.
- You may decrease your payment, yet end up paying more interest over the life of the new loan under a variety of

scenarios. Only careful, informed analysis can protect you from this.

- You become exposed to mortgage products that can cause financial troubles down the road.

The importance of removing the focus from the payment cannot be overstated. As you learn how to shop for and manage your mortgage debt, you will discover the many issues associated with buying on payment.

Manage Your Mortgage by Keeping the End in Mind

Your mind-set about home ownership and mortgage debt will drive your choices. It has a dramatic impact on how your finances look over time. The end game is to be mortgage free. This must remain in the forefront of your thinking.

Do you daydream about moving up, or are you looking to live in a home that is adequate for your needs? Are you using leverage to buy more than you really can afford, or are you trying to minimize the cost and size of your mortgage debt? Do you tap equity to supplement your lifestyle and to make fancy home improvements, or are you trying to build equity and become debt free?

If your attitude is to chase the allure of a bigger, fancier, more luxurious home than you really need, you are in for big trouble. It doesn't take a brain surgeon to determine which approach contained in the questions above makes more sense. One borrows against the future, with no concern for the long-term costs of carrying mortgage debt into the retirement years. The other looks to the future, planning for a day when there are no debts to service.

Which sounds better to you?

Ask the Right Question

The worst question you can ever ask is how much you can qualify for. This will lead you to buy too much home, or in the case of refinancing, tempt you to pull cash out of your home.

The right question is how much you can *afford*—and that's a question you must ask of yourself. Just because Fannie Mae or the FHA might allow you to borrow more than what you should spend doesn't mean you should go there. If you wish to live a quality life that leaves room for giving, saving, and spending time with people, you'd be well advised to define what you can afford, rather than to let the lender define it for you.

You need to think about today *and* tomorrow. The costs of operating your home normally rise over time; and given the rate of government spending, we will be certain to experience rapidly increasing costs as inflation begins to take hold.

> *Just because Fannie Mae or the FHA might allow you to borrow more than what you should spend doesn't mean you should go there.*

One of the things a lender examines when qualifying an applicant is the debt ratio. There are two of them.

1. The Front-End Ratio

This is the percentage of your total income that is represented by your mortgage payment (principal and interest), property taxes, and insurance. This is commonly referred to as PITI. The percentage is referred to as the debt-to-income ratio, or DTI. Front-end DTIs range from 28 percent to as high as 36 percent.

2. The Back-End Ratio

The back-end DTI is the percentage of your total income that is represented by your PITI plus all debts, including child support payments. Back-end DTIs range from 36 percent to 50 percent.

Let's look at the maximum front-end ratio for a moment. Here's how it breaks down under the Give, Save, and Live approach:

Income and Cash Outflows	Percentages
Total income	100%
Less cash outflows/expenses:	
Giving	(10%)
Saving	(10%)
Mortgage payment (PITI)	(36%)
Federal and State income taxes	(25%)
Subtotal outflows/expenses	(81%)
Net spendable cash	19%

This leaves 19 percent of your gross income to pay for the cost of running and maintaining your home, food, clothing, car payments, and maintenance/repairs and situational expenses. And these are just the *necessities!*

This also assumes you have no debts other than your mortgage and your car payments. Assume that you had such debt and pushed the back end ratio to 50 percent of your income, which is 14 percent higher than the figure in the table. *That would leave only 5 percent to cover necessities.*

Do these numbers scare you? They should!

Let's circle back to the right question: how much can you afford? I suggest that you never exceed 25 percent as a front-end DTI. To do anything more will challenge your finances by leaving very little room for savings and errors.

If this means you have to rent until you can afford a home—rent. If you are in a home and your front-end DTI exceeds 25 percent, your best bet is to get with the program, pay down all other debts, cut expenses, and try your best to create some margin in your financial life.

INSIDER VIEWPOINT:
Making Broke People Broke

Assume you had $100 million and you decided to make mortgage loans with the money. Take a look at the following loan guidelines and determine if you would lend under these conditions:

- A homebuyer can borrow up to 97 percent of the value of the home (a gift can be used as a down payment).
- The back-end DTI can go as high as 43 percent.
- No cash reserves are required (not a penny in the bank).
- The income from a person who will not live in the home can be used to help qualify for the mortgage.
- Credit scores can be as low as 600.

Would you lend your money under these circumstances? You wouldn't, but the government will use our money to do it. Concealed under the blanket of the government's affordable housing initiatives is a financial disaster waiting to happen.

The list above is a short summary of the guidelines under which the FHA will make mortgages. Does this sound affordable to you, or does it sound like government-assisted housing? These guidelines are going to make broke people broke—a 43 percent back-end DTI is only going to enslave the borrower to the home, allowing no room for savings and little hope of financial security in the future. Not to mention what's going to happen once inflation kicks in and the cost of everything one needs to live goes up.

These guidelines aren't much different than the aggressive guidelines that existed before the crash. They are as liberal as what was offered by subprime lenders, although they made these loans with funds acquired in the open market. Rightfully so, the open market has tightened credit standards. Has the government?

The government has levied heavy criticism on the subprime lending industry. Without getting into the legitimacy of finger pointing, the subprime industry was a product of the open, free market. Relaxed lending standards led to a meltdown that has the country in a tailspin. Considering what we know today, how on earth can it be right for the very government that views subprime lenders as criminals to make loans through the FHA that are riskier than what the free market will allow today? And with *our money* at that!

I'm sure you wouldn't make loans like these if you had $100 million, but you don't have a choice. Remember who pays for the federal government.

Build Your Cash Reserves

If you don't have cash reserves, you aren't going to be able to make your mortgage payments in the event of a crisis. For this reason, it's imperative that you build your cash reserves to at least six months of expenses.

If you are aggressive in paying down your mortgage debt, make sure you maintain your cash reserves while you are building equity in your home. If you lose your job or experience some other event that challenges your ability to make your mortgage payment, you are at great risk. If you have equity in your home and can't make your payment, it's a no-brainer for the lender to move swiftly to foreclosure.

INSIDER TIP:
The Credit Safety Net

The way to build a safety net is to acquire a home equity line of credit *while you have the credit to do so.* You must commit *not* to use the line for anything other than severe emergencies and you must maintain your cash reserves. If the worst case happens and you deplete your cash reserves, you'll be able to tap your home equity and turn it into much needed cash to help you save your home.

Don't Buy the Ability to Consume

The mortgage industry typically markets to, and lives off of, the never-ending quest of the consumer to lower his payments. In far too many cases, a borrower refinances a mortgage, obtains a lower payment, and then lives according to the lower payment. Refinancing simply to reduce the payment creates cash flow for additional consumption. Most borrowers have no plan for the monthly payment savings and end up spending all of it on "stuff." Worse yet, many home owners end up borrowing more from different credit sources (purchasing a new car, for example) as the capacity to take on additional payments has increased.

Every time a person refinances for the express purpose to lower his payment, he further extends the maturity date of his mortgage and buys the ability to consume at higher levels. This accomplishes nothing. It doesn't create wealth in the form of savings or home equity; all it does is extend mortgage debt well into the future, allowing the home owner to play today and pay for it tomorrow.

It should be obvious this is a serious trap, but it is far too common. You aren't saving a dime if you spend all of the monthly savings after you refinance.

Don't Get Sucked In

During the time you hold your mortgage, it is likely you will be subject to significant swings in the interest rate environment and general economy.

Your goal should be to consistently reduce the cost of your mortgage debt when interest rates cycle downward. I believe the best strategy is to lock in the cost of housing by obtaining a fixed-rate mortgage, refinancing only when fixed-rates drop low enough to justify taking a new loan. This strategy (which is covered in chapter 19) keeps things simple and will, quite frankly, keep you out of trouble.

Generally speaking, the introductory rates associated with hybrid adjustable-rate mortgages (mortgages that are fixed for a period of time and then are adjustable for the remaining term) are lower than fixed-rate products. The shorter the introductory period, the lower the rate.

The problem for consumers is the mortgage industry markets these loans aggressively during certain interest-rate cycles, which works against the better strategy of attempting to lock in the long-term cost of housing by fixing your payment. It's all too easy to get sucked into the wrong loan.

Here's what traditionally happens in downward and upward trending interest rate markets:

Downward trending

Mortgage companies will advertise their lowest rates in order to spark your interest. Those rates normally are associated with hybrid-ARM products. For example, in 2003 you would have been able to obtain a mortgage with a three-year fixed rate as low as 3.75 percent. At the same time, you would have been able to lock in a thirty-year fixed rate at 5 percent. For a $350,000 mortgage, the payment on the hybrid-ARM is $1,621 and the payment on the fixed-rate loan is $1,879—a difference of more than $250 per month. It's just too enticing to take the bait and go for the lower payment, which is great for the mortgage company because they know you'll be coming back to refinance when rates trend upward.

Upward trending

When rates are cycling upward, mortgage companies advertise the security of a fixed-rate loan to end the pain that's being experienced by borrowers who were sold hybrid ARMs. Once you get refinanced into that loan, you are on the hit list for the time interest rates cycle downward again.

INSIDER VIEWPOINT:
The Toxic Nature of ARMs

Hybrid and other adjustable-rate mortgages present many risks to home owners, most of which aren't easily managed, regardless of your level of financial knowledge. ARMs can attack your finances in the following ways:

- The lower rates tempt you to buy too much house, or borrow more than you need when refinancing.
- Borrowers become accustomed to the low payment and typically increase their borrowing and spending, leaving little room to deal with escalating mortgage payments.
- Home values may flatten or decline as rates trend upward, leaving no room to refinance, in the worst case forcing home owners into foreclosure should they be unable to afford the bigger payments.
- You may become a serial refinancer, chasing lower rates when you get past the introductory period and getting stuck each time with another thirty years of payments.
- You might not qualify for a refinance when rates increase, even if you don't lose your job or take a pay cut.

History serves as the best example of the associated risks, as we have witnessed with the collapse of the housing market.

It wouldn't be good for the mortgage industry if you stuck with the fixed-rate strategy, because you'd have little incentive to refinance when rates trend upward again. Per the Federal Reserve's Web site, conventional mortgage rates averaged approximately 9 percent from 1972 to 2008. In the example above, the hybrid-ARM payment at 9 percent would eventually be about $2,650—and that's over $1,000 more than the introductory payment!

Don't Let Them Take You to the Well

Creditors only make money by lending you money. That's obvious. But think about it for a moment: thousands of lenders of all sorts are competing for a share of your wallet. They'll find myriad ways to get you to move your debt from one to another and they'll keep you in perpetual debt if you let them.

The process starts with your very first mortgage. The larger the mortgage balance, the more income the lender will make—both in the origination process and over the term of the loan. The process of buying a home is very emotional, and if you let emotions get the better of you, you'll probably end up borrowing too much money for too much house. Even if this doesn't happen, once your mortgage is set into motion, you become part of the vast database of home owners the mortgage industry will market to.

The mortgage business, as it relates to a mortgage broker or anyone who is in the business of originating new loans, is a *transaction*-oriented business. Because of this, they must continue to make new loans to keep the cash register ringing. They are monitoring the market and will continue to solicit you to refinance for any reason they can conjure up. If you understand this motivation, it should cause you to raise your guard and make sure you understand the benefits of refinancing before you enter into a new loan. Remember that your lender probably doesn't care if you go further into debt if he can make a profit on you.

Lenders have a wide array of data available to them that allows them to pinpoint with startling accuracy which borrowers are most likely to refinance. By monitoring the value of your home, the size of your current mortgage, and your credit score, lenders are able to target customers who have the equity and credit to take out a new loan for a larger amount (remember—the larger the loan, the more the profit for the lender). If you are not careful, these alluring offers can result in ever-growing mortgage debt over time—as the value of your home and your income increases—thereby allowing you to absorb higher payments. Here is a partial list of what will cause a lender to market to you:

> *Lenders have a wide array of data available to them that allows them to pinpoint with startling accuracy which borrowers are most likely to refinance.*

- Your home has increased in value and you can refinance and take cash out for large purchases.
- Rates have decreased and your current loan was originated during a time of higher rates.
- You have credit card or other debt and a refinance will allow you to consolidate your debts into one easy payment.
- You have an adjustable-rate mortgage, rates are increasing, and a refinance will offer you the security of a fixed-rate mortgage.
- You have a fixed-rate mortgage and a new hybrid ARM will provide for lower payments.

- You've held your mortgage for three years or more. It's quite easy for the mortgage provider to lower your payment simply by writing a new thirty-year mortgage.

All of these options are marketed in a way to make you believe you'll save money or obtain other benefits—but that may not be true. The reality, again, is that lenders make a living by consistently refinancing your mortgage debt. This means they need to keep you coming back to the well. It supports the contention that the industry wants to keep you in debt and it is never going to stop soliciting you as long as you have the ability to borrow money. The best line of defense is to ignore it, understand when you should refinance, and initiate the process only when the time is right. You'll learn all about this in chapter 19.

> *Lenders make a living by consistently refinancing your mortgage debt. This means they need to keep you coming back to the well.*

Never Tap Home Equity

You must not fall into the trap of tapping home equity for the purpose of buying depreciating assets. The resulting mortgage debt, and the corresponding payments, will remain in effect long after the things you purchased become worthless. There is no wealth created by this practice, except for the retailers you bought things from.

Unfortunately, tapping home equity in order to consume is alluring. This common practice has spelled disaster for many American households. Once the excitement of the purchases wears off, the drudgery of the payments sets in. This is in stark contrast to a home owner who resisted the temptation to tap his "wealth" by pulling cash out of his home. This home owner is much better off in the long run because he is working to become mortgage free and will have significant home equity that can be used more wisely in his later years of life.

Beware of the Commissioned Salesperson

When you buy *anything*, it makes sense to understand how the person selling you the product is getting paid. If he's on commission, you are at risk of being overcharged.

This is a particularly big problem in the mortgage business, in which the vast majority of mortgage brokers, loan officers, and other salespeople get paid on a percentage of the revenue your loan produces for the lender. When option ARMs were flooding the market, they were one of the most lucrative products available to the mortgage salesperson even-though there were very few borrowers for which the product was appropriate. Is it any wonder so many of these mortgages were sold?

To make matters worse, some components of a mortgage loan provide additional revenue to the lender (and the salesperson) but work against you as a borrower. A perfect example of this is a prepayment penalty, which is a penalty of up to six months' interest if you pay the loan off before a specified period of time. You don't want a prepayment penalty, but the salesperson may be motivated to include one if it puts more money in his pocket.

It is safe to assume that the typical salesperson wishes to sell the largest loan possible with the most bells and whistles in order to maximize his income.

Your best defense, therefore, is twofold:

- Find out how your mortgage salesperson will be compensated before you buy. Be on extra alert if commissions are involved.
- Learn how to shop for a mortgage so you can sniff out who's trying to take you to the cleaners.

It's Not Personal, It's Just Business

It's your money and your decision on how much house to buy or when to refinance. You must not allow your emotions to dictate your decisions and you must realize successful salespeople do several things very well. Among them are the ability to connect on a personal level and the ability to play off your emotions.

The real estate and mortgage businesses are notorious when it comes to using benefits of the "personal relationship" for their own gain. It's not a bad thing to connect with your real estate agent or mortgage provider, but it's in your best interests to keep it solely at a business level. You are better off using the knowledge you gain in *Mind Your Own Mortgage* to remain objective.

Stick with the purpose of the transaction and nothing more.

Stick to the Plan

Make your objective simple: pay off your mortgage and avoid a mortgage crisis along the way.

Now that you have a grip on what can cause you problems, you'll find it quite simple to steer clear of trouble outside of some catastrophic event in your life. The principles are fairly simple to apply. Some of the things I've listed require study; in particular, understanding how to buy on price, how to manage your mortgage, and when to refinance. We will cover these in great detail.

Let's start by shopping for it.

SHOP FOR IT

7

Keep It Simple

John and Cynthia: Simple Is Better

John and Cynthia live in a nice neighborhood in Southern California. John has a good job, which has allowed them to realize Cynthia's dream of being a stay-at-home mom. They bought their house in 1998 and watched it skyrocket in value up until the crash.

John and Cynthia refinanced in 2001 and again in 2004, each time for the sole purpose of trading their thirty-year fixed-rate mortgage for another with a lower rate, paying very little in closing costs each time. Their current mortgage rate is 5.5 percent and they have continued to make the original payment all along and added more whenever they had the extra cash. Despite the recession, they are on track to being mortgage free by 2019—fifteen years earlier than they would be had they taken advantage of the new payment each time they refinanced.

John rejected the constant offers for rates as low as 2 percent during the mortgage boom years. He ignored the messaging to refinance, doing so only when it was in the best interests of his family's future. It's a good thing he did.

Although their home is worth far less than it was during the boom cycle, it's not nearly as underwater as any of their neighbors'. Despite a few foreclosures on their street, they don't feel the pain of the recession, nor are they worried about the value of their home. It was never meant to be an investment from which they would supplement their lifestyle.

John and Cynthia kept things simple—simpler than Alan Greenspan would have had he followed his own advice to take advantage of lower adjustable mortgage rates. Life is good when it's simple. John and Cynthia have the time and freedom to enjoy life.

Simple is better.

You Are at Risk

In order to obtain the right loan at the right price, you must learn how to shop. With the confusing and cumbersome pile of disclosures you must sign regarding your mortgage, and the lack of clarity over how it's priced, it's all too easy to get frustrated and give in to the process.

Whenever you shop for a mortgage, you are at risk of acquiring a loan at an inappropriate price that's not right for you. This happens for two reasons:

1. The more complicated the mortgage loan, the harder it is for you to understand. For example, far too many consumers have entered into mortgage loans that have low introductory payments, yet they don't understand the mechanics of how the payments are calculated, how they adjust, and the economic

circumstances that will cause their mortgage payments to increase or decrease.

2. While price is a relatively simple concept to the lender, there isn't a simple method to communicate it to the consumer, nor is there a method to communicate the range of price options within a particular loan product. It's not that there isn't a way to provide the information, it's that the mortgage industry has withheld the information from the consumer in order to prevent commodity pricing.

If the industry would allow commodity pricing, there would be little differentiation. People would shop on price instead of the manufactured benefits of relationships, perceived product features, and payment. You've been taught how the mortgage market works, so you know there are only a few entities that control underwriting standards, which drive loan products. How different can one lender be from another? After all, a mortgage is simply a pile of money.

Since differentiation between lenders must be manufactured, it stands to reason you'll be exposed to gimmicks in order to get you to sign on the dotted line.

Since differentiation must be manufactured, it stands to reason you'll be exposed to gimmicks in order to get you to sign on the dotted line. How many times have you heard low payments or rates being advertised? But what's the true price? The very focus on these elements creates an environment that leads to the wrong loan at the wrong time.

Understand What You Are Buying

Before you decide on price, you must examine the loan—because price tends to appear lower on mortgage products that present the greatest risk to the home owner.

Understanding your mortgage loan means that you are conversant with the terms of the mortgage note. These terms dictate the payment, the maturity (or payoff) date, and, if you have an adjustable-rate mortgage, the manner and timing in which the payment is subject to change.

There are such a wide variety of mortgage products offered at any point in time (which change depending upon economic conditions) that it's impractical to list them here. However, there is generally a consistent staple of fixed and adjustable-rate mortgage products that are relatively uncomplicated. I believe it's a waste of your time to consider anything other than the type of loans discussed below. And I strongly recommend that you only consider fixed-rate financing, for reasons you'll discover as you read on. If you have the right view of finances, you have no reason to deal with an exotic or adjustable-rate mortgage loan. They sound good, but they almost always lead to trouble.

As discussed in chapter 3, mortgages that are acceptable to Fannie Mae or Freddie Mac (agency standards) are referred to as *conforming loans*. This means they meet the generally higher underwriting/qualification standards of these agencies and that the loans are no greater than $417,000 for a single-family residence. In some areas of the country, there are *super-conforming loans*, which are agency loans at higher amounts to compensate for geographic differences in home values. All loans over agency amounts, or those that do not meet agency underwriting standards, are considered *nonconforming loans* and are subject to different qualification guidelines standards, depending upon the marketplace and investor appetite for these loans.

In order to simplify the discussion, conforming or nonconforming mortgage loans fall into only two categories: fixed or adjustable. The descriptions below cover the most widely available types of these loans.

Fixed-Rate Mortgages

A fixed-rate mortgage carries an interest rate that remains the same for the entire term of the mortgage; it is generally offered for fifteen-, twenty-, twenty-five-, thirty-, and forty-year loan terms. The shorter the term of the fixed-rate mortgage, the better the price will be and the larger the payment will become (notice how price and payment are inversely related).

Adjustable-Rate Mortgages (ARMs)

An adjustable-rate mortgage carries an interest rate that changes over the life of the loan, at predetermined intervals based upon a rate index. The initial mortgage payment, and all subsequent changes to the mortgage payment, are calculated based upon the payment necessary to pay the loan in full from the date of the interest-rate change to the maturity date of the mortgage. The most important features of an adjustable-rate mortgage are as follows:

- Initial interest rate: the rate that is used for the introductory period of the loan (commonly referred to as the start rate).
- The index rate: the base rate to which the margin is added to arrive at the interest rate.
- The margin: the amount that is added to the base rate to arrive at the interest rate.

- Adjustment period: the length of time between the dates on which the interest rate is changed.
- Interest rate caps: the maximum increase or decrease to the interest rate on an interest-rate adjustment date.
- Lifetime interest rate cap: the maximum rate that is allowed under the mortgage.

The most common type of adjustable-rate mortgage used by consumers in recent years is the hybrid adjustable-rate mortgage. These loans carry a fixed rate for an introductory period and are adjustable thereafter. The most common introductory periods are for one, three, or five years, but seven and ten years are also used. These loans are referred to as 1/1 ARMs, 3/1 ARMs, 5/1 ARMs, and so forth.

The shorter the introductory period, the lower the introductory rate (assuming normal market conditions). For example, a 3/1 ARM will have a fixed rate good for the first three years that is lower than the fixed rate for the first five years on a 5/1 ARM. Once the introductory period is over, however, both of these loans would be subject to similar adjustable rates and increases.

Interest-Only Adjustable-Rate Mortgages

Interest-only ARMs work exactly like hybrid ARMs, except that the payments in the fixed-rate period cover interest only. This further reduces the payment during the introductory period, but by the time the adjustments begin, it is likely you'll still owe the original balance. If your loan is fixed for five years, this means you'll now have twenty-five years to pay off the original balance of your loan instead of thirty.

Do you notice how much more complicated adjustable-rate mortgages are compared to fixed-rate mortgages? The fixed-rate loan can be described in one or two sentences!

In general, the only difference between the two is the party who assumes the interest-rate risk. With a fixed-rate loan, the lender takes the risk that rates will increase, which means the investor in the loan will make less if you don't refinance your mortgage to current rates when they are on the rise. You carry very little risk because you can always refinance if rates decline and the cost to do so is acceptable.

With an adjustable-rate mortgage, the consumer assumes the risk of interest rate adjustments. This favors the investor, as his investment will "float" with the market. While it works well in times of low interest rates, the borrower with an adjustable-rate mortgage is at greater risk overall compared to the fixed-rate mortgage loan borrower for one simple reason: when rates increase, home values generally flatten or go down (or implode, such as the case with the housing meltdown). This means the holder of the adjustable-rate mortgage may not have the equity needed to refinance into a more affordable payment. He's either going to have to come up with some money to pay down the outstanding balance and refinance or live with the payment. Even if he has the equity, he may not qualify for a new loan based on income requirements. If the existing payment is too large, he's at risk of losing his home.

When you compare your risk between the two alternatives, the fixed-rate mortgage clearly comes out on top.

By now it's obvious that I am a big fan of fixed-rate loans. I would rather have the simplicity, certainty, and security of a fixed-rate loan over the risk of an adjustable-rate loan any day of the week.

Keeping It Simple

The beauty of keeping it simple is that it keeps you out of trouble. I can either afford the fixed-rate payment or I can't. I don't need to worry about the complexities of an adjustable-rate mortgage or an exotic mortgage. I'm not squeezing into a loan that might come back to bite me later, and my shopping experience is going to be much easier, since there are fewer terms associated with the loan. I don't have to be concerned about future rate increases and the possibility of being stuck with a payment I cannot afford. At the same time, if interest rates decline, I can reduce the cost of my mortgage debt by refinancing into another fixed-rate mortgage.

Simply stated, I *understand* and can *comprehend* what I'm getting into.

There's another very important benefit: whenever I make additional payments toward principal, I know exactly what I'll save and how much earlier I'll pay off my mortgage, because my interest rate isn't subject to change. When you do the same thing with an adjustable-rate mortgage, you'll have no idea what the benefits will be since you can't count on the rate.

My advice is therefore to always stick with fixed-rate financing. This is the first and most important step to keeping your financial life simple and certain.

Don't Let Anyone Talk You Out of It
Charles and Emily: Sticking to Their Guns

The offer looked fantastic: a new mortgage at 4 percent and a $300 reduction in the monthly payment. Charles and Emily bought a home just a couple years ago, with little money down under an FHA loan program. Their rate is fixed for thirty years at 5.875 percent.

Charles and Emily work for a nonprofit organization that provides aid to orphans in foreign countries. This is their life's work—the purpose for which they have been placed on this planet.

Their friend in the mortgage business offered them a new 4 percent loan, which is fixed for five years and then goes adjustable. Their friend offered the following incentives: they'll save $18,000 on the loan payments alone in the first five years, and they can refinance later into another fixed-rate loan if rates go up.

Pretty standard advice for what is a very dangerous loan for Charles and Emily. The problems?

First, their income is essentially fixed; it'll rise modestly, if at all, over the next five years. They just managed to qualify for their existing loan. If rates increase, there is a high likelihood they will not qualify for a refinance. Additionally, inflation is sure to spike interest rates sharply upward at some time in the next several years, exposing them to steadily increasing rates and, correspondingly, a steadily increasing mortgage payment—to levels they will not be able to afford.

Their friend is handing them a ticking time bomb. Did we mention the closing costs for this loan were 3 percent of the loan amount ($9,000)? Add that to the new loan balance, thank you.

Fortunately, Charles and Emily said no thank you. They're sticking to their guns (and looking for a new friend).

You will be met with resistance if you make the choice to stick with fixed-rate financing. Mind your own mortgage and don't let anyone change it for you! Fixed-rate mortgages *appear* to be more expensive than adjustable-rate mortgages, which carry low introductory rates. Since you can't predict interest rates, you can't depend on the lower rate to extend into the future.

Here's a fact: the industry can't predict interest rates either. Mortgage pricing is constructed in a way that reflects this truth. Here's how:

- The shorter the expected term of a mortgage, the lower the interest rate. The expected term is the average amount of time a borrower will hold a mortgage, and the payoff of your mortgage prior to its expected maturity date is referred to as the prepayment date.
- Other things being equal, a thirty-year fixed-rate loan is expected to be held by the borrower for a longer period of time, hence the investor requires a greater rate of return to compensate for the additional time his money is tied up. On average, the industry expects you'll hold a fixed-rate mortgage for seven years. Conversely, it is much more likely you will refinance a three-year hybrid ARM once the adjustment period begins and payment shock sets in.
- The lower rates associated with loans that have shorter prepayment dates reflect the fact that neither you nor the investor can count on introductory interest rate benefits to extend into the future.

If the industry doesn't count on the longevity of the lower rates associated with an adjustable-rate mortgage, why should you? That fixed-rate mortgage might seem more expensive, but in the vast majority of circumstances, it won't be. Stick to your guns and stick with a fixed-rate.

Let's Make the Point Clear

There are many risks associated with coming off your high horse and succumbing to the allure of an adjustable-rate mortgage. I've mentioned these earlier and one is worth reemphasizing at this point.

Your spending habits are likely connected to the size of your mortgage payment. For the period of time your payments are low, you are much more likely to increase your spending and your borrowing, since your lower payment allows you to do so. As you become accustomed to your nifty mortgage payment and you spend what's left over like it's never going to change, you diminish your ability to cope with rising interest rates. If you have no savings, your margin for error becomes very slim. You might increase your borrowing and spending to the point that you will be unable to qualify for a new mortgage to bail you out when rates increase.

Here's a real-life example. A friend of mine has a 5/1 interest-only ARM. This loan carries a fixed rate in the first five years because the payments are interest-only; they are adjustable for the remaining twenty-five years. He originally borrowed $520,000 at 5.375 percent and his interest-only payment for the first five years was $2,329. Interest rates have decreased since he acquired this loan, so along came the adjustment date after the fifth year and he was pleased to find his rate was adjusted from 5.375 percent to 4.375 percent.

Isn't that great news? If it were, why did his payment increase to $2,854 for $525 more per month?

It's because he still owes the original balance of $520,000—but he now has only twenty-five years to pay off the loan, instead of thirty. My friend became accustomed to the lower payment and was oblivious to the risk. He didn't go on a spending spree, nor did he acquire additional debt, but his financial situation had deteriorated due to general economic circumstances, and his house didn't have enough equity to allow a refinance. Now he is stuck.

Had my friend obtained a fixed-rate mortgage five years ago, he would have probably borrowed less, he would have been paying down principal, and he would have a payment he could count on.

INSIDER VIEWPOINT:
Eight Percent Is Great

There are many who will disagree with the points I've made about using ARMs. Many mortgage advisors believe it is worth the risk to play the market, switching from ARMs to fixed and vice versa, depending on market conditions. These advisors are normally the same people who are selling you the loan, so you must question the validity of the advice.

Here's the bottom line: 8 percent is a great fixed mortgage rate. Rates have been low for so long that it's affected our perspective. The following chart depicts conventional mortgage rates published by the Federal Reserve from 1972 to 2009:

Historical Average Conventional Mortgage Rates

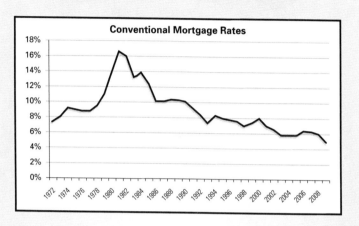

It only takes a quick look to conclude that 8 percent is the historical average between the wild swings caused by the inflation of the early 1980s and the artificial lows seen today. It's therefore fair to conclude anything below 6 percent is excellent and that it's not worth it to gamble.

As a matter of fact, those holding adjustable-rate mortgages are sitting on a ticking time bomb. The rate of government spending during the recession of 2008 and beyond is sure to cause inflation in the near future. If it gets anywhere near as bad as it did in the early 1980s, you'd better run—because the fuse is going to burn fast.

8

Prepare for a Fight

Pat: Empowered and Equipped

Pat is a great steward of his family's finances. He does his best to sock money away and hasn't ventured into being overleveraged.

Pat thought he knew a fair bit about mortgages and felt he could carry his weight negotiating with mortgage brokers. He never let the personal side of the equation interfere with what is purely a financial transaction.

But he's discovered something new lately. After learning about the Mind Your Own Mortgage Shopping System and taking a stance to implement it, he's met with resistance he hadn't encountered on previous occasions. "It's like going back thirty years, walking into the car dealership, and demanding to see the dealer invoice," Pat says. "They wouldn't have given up the information, but things changed. Now it's time for the mortgage world to change."

Pat feels empowered. As soon as he meets resistance, he knows something's up—and it's not in his favor. It's like a grand awakening—

and now the cart is driving the horse. He's fully equipped to turn the tables on a game he never knew existed.

What if I told you a mortgage quote should look like this:

Loan Amount	Term/Type	Rate	Total Cost
$375,000	30-Year Fixed	5.25%	$3,200

How simple is *that*? Have you ever been presented with a quote that looks like this? Notice that the monthly payment is conspicuously missing. We'll get to it in a later chapter, but I didn't present the payment so I could make a point: price is about your rate and the total cost to obtain the rate. It's no more complicated than that. The payment has nothing to do with it.

Now let's assume you have two quotes. Which of the following is better?

Lender	Loan Amount	Term/Type	Rate	Total Cost
Alpha	$375,000	30-Year Fixed	5.25%	$3,200
Omega	$375,000	30-Year Fixed	5.25%	$2,450

Can you tell who has the better price? This is how it should be, but it's not. Do you think the industry wants this kind of clarity and simplicity? Why, before you know it, lenders would be forced to compete on price and profit margins would be squeezed. Perhaps this would require the industry to become more efficient, further spurring competition and driving down costs; savings that could be passed on to the consumer. We wouldn't want that now, would we?

One loan is better to the tune of $750, yet the payments on these loans are *exactly the same*. This makes it easy to hide the truth about price, lining Alpha's pockets whenever someone doesn't check out Omega.

This type of transparency *is* available, given you know how to ask for it. I have developed a shopping system that will enable you to obtain quotes just like the examples shown above. The system will allow you to sniff out the best mortgage provider (on price) before you commit to anyone. This shopping system involves collecting information that is available (but not normally provided) and summarizing the information in a manner that makes determining the best price as easy as determining who has the lowest gas prices in town.

The Mind Your Own Mortgage Shopping System (MYOM Shopping System) takes a bit of work. That's to be expected because if it didn't, there wouldn't be a need for it. The work will pay off because you will have obtained the information necessary to force commodity price presentation in an industry that refuses to provide clarity and transparency. Consider it your own consumer revolution.

If you want to engage in the revolution, you must first prepare for the fight. The mortgage broker or loan officer and the companies they work for are going to resist. The good news is you are on the offense: you can demand the information. They will be required to provide it if they want your business. And they will yield to your forces of knowledge.

I am going to teach you how to use the MYOM Shopping System. Before you step into the ring, let's make sure you are fully prepared.

The Typical Mortgage Experience

Let's take a look at the typical process the consumer endures to obtain a quote and move forward with obtaining a loan. Here's how it goes down:

> **DAVE'S FRIEND PETE:** Hey pal, I just refinanced my mortgage and I saved 450 bucks per month. I know you've been thinking of refinancing your mortgage. I worked with this guy Chris at ABC Mortgage. They had great rates and my payment . . . well, it's $450 less than it was before. Here's Chris's number—give him a call and I'm sure he'll take great care of you.
>
> **DAVE DIALS THE NUMBER—CHRIS ANSWERS:** Thank you for calling ABC Mortgage. My name is Chris. How can I help you today?
>
> **DAVE:** Hello, Chris. I got your number from my friend Pete. He said you made him a great deal on his refinance. I was wondering what you could do for me.
>
> **CHRIS:** That's right! Pete's a super guy. How do you know him?
>
> **DAVE:** He and I have been friends since high school.
>
> **CHRIS:** That's great. Where'd you go to high school?
>
> **DAVE:** Right here in my hometown.
>
> **CHRIS:** Wow. That's great. You still live in the town where you went to high school and stayed connected with guys like Pete. You're fortunate to have a friend like that. Most of us move around too much and miss out on stuff like that.
>
> Let's see what I can do for you. Tell me about your

current mortgage. How much do you owe and what's your monthly payment?

DAVE: Well, I owe about $370,000 and my payment is $2,400 per month.

CHRIS: Hmmm. What's your interest rate?

DAVE: It's six and one-quarter percent.

CHRIS: I think I can help you with this. I'm sure we can lower that payment for you and I believe I can get you a better rate than you are currently paying. Your situation sounds a lot like Pete's, and we got him a great deal. Let me take down some information so we can get started.

Now that Chris has established rapport and has Dave interested, he proceeds to get some basic information. The attention has been directed toward payment reduction. Chris has Dave's time and attention—Dave is invested in the phone call. Dave agrees to complete an application over the phone. Chris tells him that he must run his credit report in order to provide a good rundown of the options, so Dave tells Chris to go ahead. Chris asks for a day so he can do the homework and come up with the best possible deal. Dave acquiesces and Chris calls back the very next day:

CHRIS: Hello there! I've got some great news for you, Dave. Are you ready for this? You told me you owe $370,000, your current rate is 6.25 percent, and your mortgage payment is $2,400 per month. I can lower your rate to 5.375 percent, and this is without points. In addition, I can lower your payment to $2,100 per month, saving you $300.

DAVE: That sounds pretty good, but I was hoping to save a little bit more.

CHRIS: Well, I guess you can shop around and submit an application to another lender, but I've just quoted you a rate that's almost 1 percent lower than you are paying today. That's going to be hard to beat. Plus, I'm going to save you $300 a month.

Let me ask you this. If I put $300 in an envelope and placed it under your front doormat each month, would you take it?

DAVE: Uh. Sure, I would! Why not?

CHRIS (now with conviction): Exactly! Why wouldn't you? I worked this out with my manager and I think we've got a great deal for you. And guess what? If you go ahead with this and interest rates decrease, we'll give you the lower rate. Does that sound good?

The deal sounds good to Dave, so he agrees to proceed. Chris is excited for Dave and congratulates him. Chris has closed the sale while providing very little information. He's not going to show Dave any pricing options, since he has him right where he wants him.

The next step is to begin the loan process. Chris collects $350 to pay for an appraisal, which will be refunded when the loan closes. A few days later Dave receives a Good Faith Estimate (the GFE). The Good Faith Estimate has all kinds of numbers on it for a variety of fees that make it look like one hundred people are involved in the loan and need to be paid. Chris walks Dave through all the various fees that are necessary to make the loan happen. The lender charges some and third parties charge others. Chris explains he can't do anything about third-party fees because they pass through from the various vendors, like the title and escrow companies. They are a necessary component to complete the loan, so Dave decides not to bother with them.

Dave thinks this is pretty complicated, but Chris seems like a nice guy, he took care of Pete, and he's giving him a quote in good faith. Since faith means Dave is counting on a promise, he might as well count on a nice guy.

When it's all said and done, the lender and third-party fees amount to $5,500, which will be added to Dave's loan balance. But he's saving $300 per month, so he decides to proceed.

In reality, all Dave has received to this point is a Good Faith Estimate. He hasn't been given a guarantee or written promise of any kind. Dave is entering into the largest financial transaction of his life based solely on a Good Faith Estimate with a guy he doesn't know. He's at the mercy of the commissioned salesperson.

Let's roll the clock forward and take note of what happens next:

- Chris introduces Dave to the loan processor and steps out of the picture. She's going to help coordinate the paperwork, but if there are questions, Chris will be there to help. Now the mountain of paperwork begins. Dave has already invested substantial time, so he feels as if he has no choice but to keep plugging away.
- As the weeks pass by, a few things have changed from the original quote. The appraisal on Dave's home didn't come in as expected and his debt-to-income ratios are a little out of whack. Chris needs to add 0.75 percent to the loan charges, increasing them by $2,775. The difference in the monthly payment is negligible, so it's not that big of a deal.
- Chris calls one day with a great sense of urgency. Interest rates have moved upward since Dave applied and he needs

to lock his loan. Dave chose to float his rate because Chris promised him a lower rate at closing if rates went down. Well, rates went up! Chris never mentioned anything about rates going up.

- Dave's rate increases by one-eighth of a percent to 5.5 percent, and the payment is now $2,145. That's still $255 less than he was paying before. Free money under Dave's doormat, right?
- It's time to sign loan documents. The process might have been frustrating, but Dave can't take the time to start over with someone else. Dave signs on the dotted line, with a little remorse, but he's glad it's over.

This example contains the most common mistakes made by mortgage shoppers. Most people aren't aware of these mistakes because they haven't been educated and therefore enter the process ill-equipped and uninformed. We're going to change that!

The main problem with the typical process is that you aren't given an accurate, complete view of price before you are asked to proceed. Take another look at the story above. Notice the entire pitch is designed to take your eye off the ball by speaking to how much you'll save on your payment.

What Went Wrong?

Let's analyze the conversations and note where Dave went wrong:

- He became interested because Pete told him he saved $450 per month. That's starting off on the wrong foot, since Dave is now focused on the wrong thing—his payment.

- Chris directs the conversation, leading Dave. It's not the other way around. This gives Chris the upper hand from the word *go*.

- Chris is leading his horse to water (and that horse is going to drink). Notice the first question is "How much do you owe and what is your monthly payment?" Chris establishes the basis of the sale without speaking to the terms of the sale.

- When Chris comes back, he hits Dave in his soft spot. The conversation is all about how much Dave will save. This happens to fit nicely with Dave's frame of mind going in.

- The savings look good to Dave. So good that he doesn't bother to ask for the details before proceeding. Chris isn't charging Dave points, which further deflects Dave's attention. How does Dave know he's getting the best rate at no points? The sad reality is, Dave has no idea.

- The floating rate option sounds good to Dave—yet another deflection, turning Dave's focus on the opportunity to save some money if rates go down.

- Dave hasn't set a baseline with the lender, so when the price changes down the road, he's caught by surprise. While underwriting can reveal issues that will cause a change in pricing, Dave hasn't set an expectation to explain these changes in reference to the original quote.

- Dave didn't ask for a guarantee on any part of the quote.

- Dave didn't examine the quote details before he committed to the deal. The lender has three days to deliver the Good Faith Estimate, but that doesn't preclude Dave from demanding it before he proceeds.

- Dave has done no analysis of the time it will take to recoup the closing costs. His refinance could cost him more than his old loan should he move before those costs are recovered.

- Dave left it up to Chris to determine when to lock his rate, and he didn't inquire about the company's rate-lock policy. He let Chris gamble with his money and Chris lost.
- Dave parted with $350 based upon his desire to lower his payment, without shopping, comparing, and determining the best price.

Doesn't it amaze you that a home owner will enter into the largest financial transaction of his life based only on a Good Faith Estimate, with no written promise or guarantee of any kind? It's like buying a car, driving it home, and waiting for the dealership to call you weeks from now to tell you how much the car is going to cost you. Would you do that?

You wouldn't! And you shouldn't with your mortgage.

Prepared for the Fight

There aren't any disclosures given by lenders that make it easy for you to obtain price information, make comparisons, and shop for the best deal. That's by design, and they will resist if you try to circumvent convention by demanding the information you need.

This isn't necessarily bad news. Any lender who fights you will back down if he wants your business, and if he doesn't, you'll know he's not on the up-and-up.

There's not much you can do about the mortgage process, but there is a lot you can do before you commit to a lender. The MYOM Shopping System gives you the ability to control the shopping process and neutralize the lenders by forcing decisions based on price.

Before you engage, you need to keep a few things in mind:

1. Adjust your frame of mind.

Think about shopping as a fact-finding mission. Remain completely objective in your pursuit, which makes sense because you are shopping a commodity. There is nothing to lose, since you can always walk away from the bargaining table.

2. Stick to your guns.

The very first step, before considering anything else, is to examine the loan and understand how it works. Payment or rate does not enter into the picture—if you look at these first, you will be attracted to the loan before you understand what it's all about. This part's easy, because you are going to stick with fixed-rate financing.

3. Make it about price.

Price comes before payment. Why? Because if you make it about the payment, you'll get suckered into a bad loan (or a good loan at a bad price). In addition, the costs you'll pay to obtain your mortgage will be rolled into your new loan balance. That means you'll pay for any extra charges for the next thirty years, courtesy of your new loan payment.

4. Don't commit.

You aren't going to commit to anyone, no matter how good the deal sounds or how hard the sales agent tries to instill a sense of urgency to get you to buy. You are going to hold out until you obtain all that is necessary to compare price among at least three lenders.

5. Be a cautious optimist.

I don't want to convey the impression that everyone in the mortgage industry is out to take advantage of you. The price problem is rooted in age-old practices that have led to a lack of transparency. These practices might create resistance while you attempt to obtain the information you need because the industry is not used to providing it and no one asks for it. You might even run into situations in which the salesperson doesn't understand what you are asking for because his company doesn't price its loans in the format you need to enable comparison shopping. Nonetheless, you must obtain the information. Assume the lender is your opponent so you won't succumb to sales tactics. Be relentless in your pursuit, cautious along the way, and optimistic that you will prevail.

Stepping into the Ring

Once you step into the ring, there is a protocol to follow. A prizefighter has a modus operandi built upon knowledge of the opponent and a plan to break him down until he gives in or is knocked out.

Let's hope all you need to do is get him to give in (we don't want to hurt anybody).

The MYOM Shopping Process consists of the following steps:

1. Decide on the type of loan in advance—keep it simple and stick with fixed-rate financing.
2. Complete an application with at least three lenders.
3. Obtain the price for each.
4. Compare prices.

These steps *must* be completed before you commit your business to anyone. Your goal is to defuse your opponent and force commodity pricing. Deploying these steps will neutralize the lender because you are engaged *only* in an exercise to extract price. It cuts out the chatter—the typical gimmicks and sales tactics used to commit you to the process before you've done your homework.

The MYOM Shopping System *forces the lender to give in.* That's great news! Didn't we say we didn't want to hurt anybody?

In order to make best use of the system, I've compiled a list of the top ten tactics to keep in mind as you engage:

1. Deal only with lenders worthy of your business.

Technology has enabled lenders to provide accurate price quotes, given the information and assumptions contained in the standard mortgage loan application. This technology is referred to as *automated underwriting and pricing.* The trouble is many mortgage brokers and lenders haven't made the investment to properly leverage available technology. A savvy mortgage lender uses automated underwriting and computer-based pricing tables. These lenders can provide a quote at the point of sale—which means they can submit your application and obtain a quote while you wait (and they'll be able to provide the completed MYOM Shopping System forms as well).

These lenders are in the minority, and it's easy to tell who's savvy and who's not. Many small lenders and mortgage brokers won't have the technology to provide you with a point-of-sale quote. That's okay because any lender worth his salt can at least get back to you on the very same day that you applied. If he can't, it's not worth waiting.

INSIDER TIP:

Automated Underwriting

Automated underwriting is most commonly available as a tool to mortgage lenders when writing agency and government loans.

Back in the heyday before the crash, there was a plethora of alternative mortgage products available. Most of these products had to be approved manually, since it wasn't cost effective to develop automated underwriting engines for the most creative types of financing.

With the advent of the meltdown, automated underwriting will likely take hold for the long term. This works in your favor, because it makes it easy to for the lender to provide a point-of-sale quote, and it allows the MYOM Shopping System to exploit the opportunity to demand transparency.

---

2. Turn the tables.

Go ahead and play the game with the loan officer. It's good to establish rapport, but that doesn't automatically establish trust. A good salesperson knows how to convert rapport into trust—it's what gives him the psychological edge and increases your propensity to commit.

Establishing rapport requires an investment of your time. A good salesperson knows this and will use the time you've invested as another tool to commit you to the sale.

You are a price-hunting machine—but you're human too. Turn the tables. Establish rapport and then use it to get the information you need. Remember, the salesperson has invested his time and wants something for it. Make him work for it.

3. Don't openly engage in the attack.

I've used the metaphor of battle to underscore what you're up against, but that doesn't mean you should openly engage in an attack. Be stealthy about it. Use your personality to get what you want, quietly resisting the salesperson's attempts to sell what he wants. If there's going to be a conflict, let the salesperson create it. By doing so, you'll instinctively know what you're dealing with and it'll be easier to walk away.

4. The lender must commit to provide the information.

The MYOM Shopping System uses information the lender has on hand to provide you with a quote. It's threatening because it's comprehensive and it breaks convention. You'll be provided with all the forms you need, which you must supply to the lender before you allow him to take your application. If the lender will not commit to providing the information in the format requested, do not proceed. The lender does not deserve your business.

5. Know the Big Three.

There are three factors that have the greatest influence on qualification and price:

- Your credit score
- Your income
- The value of your home

Your credit score can be obtained by the lender via inquiry. Contrary to popular belief, mortgage credit inquiries have little impact on your credit score. Generally speaking, multiple mortgage inquiries within a fourteen-day period count as only one inquiry.

Have your income information at your fingertips (like your pay stub) when you apply for a mortgage and make sure you have a good idea of the value of your home. Err on the conservative side when it comes to the latter.

6. Complete a full application.

If the lender or mortgage broker has committed to providing the MYOM Shopping System information within no more than one business day and if you feel objectively comfortable, proceed by completing a full mortgage application. This will give you the most accurate quote possible.

INSIDER TIP:
In Addition to the Big Three

You'll need other information in addition to the Big Three to complete the application. Lenders will use what is known as the Uniform Residential Mortgage Loan Application (also known as Form 1003 by mortgage professionals) to take your application.

Included in appendices at www.mindyourownmortgage.com is an example of Form 1003. I suggest you complete the following sections of the form before you begin to shop:

I. Property Information and Purpose of Loan
II. Borrower Information
III. Employment Information
IV. Monthly Income and Combined Housing Expense Information
V. Assets and Liabilities

Completing this form in advance will streamline the shopping process since you'll have all the answers you need at your fingertips.

Log onto www.mindyourownmortgage.com for forms and related guidance.

7. Make the lender give you a quote.

Don't let anyone tell you he can't give you a complete, fair, or accurate quote. If you have the credit to qualify, the lender can give you a quote based upon the assumptions contained in your mortgage application.

8. Remember that your salesperson doesn't know which way rates are heading.

More often than not, mortgage salespeople will speak to the interest-rate market as a means to the end—closing the deal. Don't get caught up in such discussions. Your mortgage salesperson doesn't have a clue which way interest rates are heading! Anyone who *does* (including you) should be trading bonds and in a very short time won't have to work for a living. If you encounter a salesperson who consistently predicts interest movements with accuracy, let's rescue him from his sorry job and buy a seat on the Chicago Board of Trade!

9. There's no need to meet face-to-face.

With today's technology, there is no need to meet face-to-face to apply for a loan. Performing your shopping duties over the phone gives you an advantage—it depersonalizes the transaction. Not that I suggest being rude, but it's much easier to hang up on someone than it is to kick him out of the house once he's made it past sticking his foot in your door.

10. Get it done in one day.

Because interest rates can change on a daily basis, you need to obtain your quotes on the same day. Let's assume you obtain quotes from three lenders. Not all of them may be able to provide a quote within minutes of completing the application. Besides, you are requesting your price quotes in a special format. Complete the applications for each lender on the same day and have them return the MYOM Shopping System quote forms to you with the price as of the following business day.

The bottom line is to obtain the information you need to make an informed decision and stay on the alert so you can sniff out impropriety. Resist all efforts to present you with a one- or two-dimensional "price" involving only rate or payment. Resist any attempt to get you to commit to the sale. Stay focused on the objective: obtaining the information you need to compare price among at least three lenders. Refuse to accept anything less than the information you ask for.

Stay True to the Objective

The following checklist serves as a handy tool for your shopping expedition. Use it as a reminder of what you need to know going in, how to engage while shopping, and what to obtain.

	The MYOM Mortgage Shopping Checklist www.mindyourownmortgage.com
✓	**A) Get ready to shop:**
	1. Adjust your frame of mind—this is a fact-finding mission
	2. Stick to your guns
	3. Make it about price
	4. Don't commit
	5. Be a cautious optimist
✓	**B) Use your tactics while shopping (reread the top ten):**
	1. Deal only with lenders worthy of your business
	2. Turn the tables
	3. Don't openly engage in the attack
	4. The lender must commit to provide the information
	5. Know the "big three"
	6. Complete a full application
	7. Make the lender give you a quote
	8. Remember your salesperson doesn't know which way rates are headed
	9. There's no need to meet face-to-face
	10. Get it done in one day
✓	**C) Perform the following in order to shop:**
	1. Select several lenders to interview
	2. Explain what type of loan you are after
	3. Show the lender the MYOM Shopping System forms and gain the lender's commitment to complete the quote in the format provided
	4. Complete a full mortgage application with the lender
	5. Request all quotes as of the same business day
	6. Request the following to be returned with your quote:
	—The lender's copy of the completed mortgage application
	—All of the MYOM Shopping System forms
	—The Good Faith Estimate
	—Written rate-lock policy
	7. Compare quotes and determine the best price

A few comments about the MYOM Mortgage Shopping Checklist are in order:

- Reread the relevant items under sections A and B from this chapter; check them off as a mental exercise to help commit them to memory.
- Go for plain vanilla, fixed-rate financing.
- All of your quotes must be obtained on the same business day because rates are subject to change on a daily (and sometimes intraday) basis. If you can't obtain the quote the same day you hold the conversations with the lenders, request the quotes to be supplied as of the next business day.
- The job will go faster if you complete the mortgage application form in advance and click off the answers over the phone during your conversation.
- Details concerning the use of the forms, the Good Faith Estimate, rate locks, and other information associated with section C are contained in the ensuing text.
- Everything under section C must be checked off of the list before you commit your business to anyone—and you don't have to pay a dime to obtain the information. If you encounter too much opposition, just walk away.

Now we're ready to shop! Let's get into the process, which begins with obtaining the price and ends with comparing quotes.

Log on to www.mindyourownmortgage.com

Everything you need to utilize the MYOM Shopping System is available at www.mindyourownmortgage.com.

The Web site contains a host of tools and resources related to this book, including automation of the MYOM Shopping System. For example, you can e-mail the forms to your lender while you are shopping over the phone, and your lender can deliver your quotes to your personal, secure account.

At www.mindyourownmortgage.com, you can shop, manage, and learn how to pay off your mortgage debt by utilizing tools that are customized to your specific situation.

9

IT'S A GALLON OF GAS!

David: Having a Hard Time Sorting It Out

David's been shopping for a new mortgage and he's plain frustrated. With a degree in finance, he figured he'd be able to make heads or tails out of the many forms and disclosures provided during the shopping process.

He is able to resist the call to action on the part of the salesperson—to David, *any pressure* is a red flag. It's just that he can't quite seem to get the straight story from the folks he's been talking to, and all he's trying to accomplish is to refinance into a plain vanilla thirty-year mortgage! This shouldn't be difficult, right?

David needs a tool to cut through to the bottom line. He hadn't learned how to shop mortgages when he was working on that finance degree.

Then David's wife brings home *Mind Your Own Mortgage*. He'll be calling the lender with the best deal tomorrow.

The end result of your shopping exercise will be a price quote that comprises two numbers: the rate and the associated total cost. That's no more complicated than the price of a gallon of gas, but it's going to take some work to boil it down to this level of simplicity.

The tools you'll use to obtain the price are simple, but it's important you learn how the end result is constructed. So we're going to build the MYOM Shopping System forms by using an example. The knowledge you'll gain will empower you to make wise, informed decisions. You're going to run ahead of the crowd and become immune to the typical affliction that causes other mortgage shoppers to limp along: deciding based upon the payment.

Empowering the Shopping Process

There are many pieces that make up price, but they can be simplified and presented in a manner that will allow you to make a good decision. Your job as a mortgage shopper is to require the lender to present your offer in a format that fits your standard. The MYOM Shopping System provides the standard with the following shopping forms:

- MYOM Rate Sheet Quote
- MYOM Quote Detail
- MYOM Quote Comparison

These forms are presented in the appendices at www.mindyourown-mortgage.com.

The MYOM Rate Sheet Quote empowers the shopping process in the following ways:

- *It reveals all price options.*

The rate sheet quote provides you with what is known as the lender's internal "retail rate sheet" for a particular loan. You are therefore able to review all of the interest rate options for your loan on one sheet of paper.

- *It filters out the noise.*

By simplifying the presentation, you are able to easily review and compare among lenders, rather than becoming lost in the details of the various charges contained in the typical loan disclosures.

- *It helps curb price manipulation.*

You are most subject to price manipulation when a salesperson is commissioned on and is empowered to set price. As you'll discover, using the MYOM Shopping System will make it difficult for your loan agent to manipulate price.

- *It reveals price the same way your mortgage provider sets price.*

The rate sheet quote is a summary of how the retail rate sheet is assembled by your mortgage provider. It's like peering into their computer system.

In this chapter, we're going to build and explain the contents of the MYOM Rate Sheet Quote and related fee detail forms.

You are most subject to price manipulation when a salesperson is commissioned on and is empowered to set price.

The Four Elements of Price

The four elements of price are universal to all mortgage loans. Because the MYOM Rate Sheet Quote Form collects these elements, it can be employed across the entire spectrum of mortgage products.

As discussed in chapter 8, after you've spoken to your lender and gained his commitment to provide your quote using the MYOM Shopping System forms, you'll complete a full mortgage application. In doing so, you'll provide the main ingredients that go into determining what loan programs (loan types) you qualify for and the price for each program. They are:

- Your credit (FICO) score
- Your income and debts
- The estimated value of your home

The combination of these factors and their impact on price is complex, subject to change depending on market circumstances, and beyond the scope of this text. There is no point in understanding these complexities; all that matters is that you obtain several quotes based on the four elements of price. It's just like buying a car—you don't have to understand the intricacy of price based upon the construction of the car; you merely need to know the price of the car.

The four elements of price for your mortgage are:

1. Rate
2. Points
3. Lender fees
4. Third-party fees

A Note About Price

All price figures used in this text are intended solely as an example of the information collected using the MYOM Shopping System. The figures are not intended to imply actual rates or fees for a mortgage, since these factors fluctuate over time. The information provided in the text should therefore not be used for the purposes of comparing price in the open marketplace.

For purposes of illustration, 6 percent has been used as the baseline rate within this text. Current average mortgage rates could be lower (or higher) than this baseline rate, but this does not affect the examples in this text, as the elements of price are constant, regardless of the interest rate environment.

The MYOM Rate Sheet Quote

Now is the time to examine how the four price elements are baked into the MYOM Rate Sheet Quote. The collection of these price elements is essential to constructing a simplified mortgage quote. We are going to build a MYOM Rate Sheet Quote from the ground up. We'll assume the following for our example (explanations are provided where necessary):

- Loan Amount: $300,000
- Loan Purpose: refinance
- Loan Type: conventional

This represents the type of loan you are shopping for. Typical loan types include Conventional Conforming, Super Conforming, Jumbo, FHA, and VA.

- Term in Years: thirty
- Amortization Type: fixed

    This represents the manner in which interest is applied to your loan. Typical amortization types include fixed, adjustable, interest-only, hybrid ARMs (such as 3/1 ARM, 5/1 ARM, 7/1 ARM, and 10/1 ARM), interest-only hybrid ARMs (such as 3/1 ARM, 5/1 ARM, 7/1 ARM, and 10/1 ARM), and regular ARMs (loans which are adjustable and have no fixed-rate introductory period).

- Escrows/Impounds: none

    An account used for the payment of property taxes and home owner's insurance. With an escrow, your monthly payment will include principal, interest, taxes, and insurance. Without one, your payment includes only principal and interest and you pay tax and insurance bills on your own.

- Lock term: thirty days

    Represents the period of time your interest rate will remain locked.

- Cash out: none

    Certain limits apply to the amount of cash allowed to be returned to the borrower after the loan closes. This is referred to as a "no cash out" loan. If you exceed the limits, the mortgage becomes a "refinance cash out."

It stands to reason the assumptions must be exactly the same for each quote you obtain. Using different assumptions will impact price and therefore invalidate your price comparisons.

In order to simplify the information in this important chapter, let's defer the necessary discussion to help you better understand escrows/impounds, rate locks, and details concerning cash-out versus no-cash-out mortgages to later in the text.

The assumptions outlined above and the four price elements at the "retail par rate" are expressed in the rate sheet quote as follows (certain fields have been left intentionally blank):

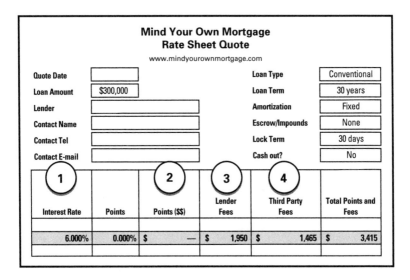

		Mind Your Own Mortgage			
		Rate Sheet Quote			
		www.mindyourownmortgage.com			

Quote Date		Loan Type		Conventional
Loan Amount	$300,000	Loan Term		30 years
Lender		Amortization		Fixed
Contact Name		Escrow/Impounds		None
Contact Tel		Lock Term		30 days
Contact E-mail		Cash out?		No

1		**2**	**3**	**4**	
			Lender	Third Party	Total Points and
Interest Rate	Points	Points ($$)	Fees	Fees	Fees
6.000%	0.000%	$ —	$ 1,950	$ 1,465	$ 3,415

The retail par rate (or *zero point rate*) is the lender's baseline rate for the loan you've requested. It is derived from the profit the lender intends to make on your loan, which is impacted by the markup from wholesale to retail interest rates. It is from this point all other rate options are priced (you'll see this as you read on). Don't concern yourself with the markup, or how much the lender is going to make on your loan. The amount of markup can vary from lender to lender, depending upon their access to the best wholesale rates. You don't need to understand interest rate markups to effectively shop for your mortgage because your shopping exercise will reveal the best retail price among the lenders you consider.

INSIDER TIP:
What the Broker Makes

When you obtain your loan from a mortgage broker, the broker is required to disclose his markup from wholesale rates. This number is known as *yield spread premium*, or YSP, and it represents the amount the lender (who is actually making the loan) is paying the mortgage broker. The YSP on a loan, while nice to know, shouldn't impact your decision as to whether to use a mortgage broker or direct lender. What matters is who has the best price.

Some mortgage brokers might extol the virtue of transparency, pointing to the fact they are disclosing how much they'll make on your loan. Don't let this influence your decision—it's completely irrelevant!

Let's review the four price elements, which are numbered in the quote sheet for easy reference:

1. Rate:

   The interest rate for your loan.
2. Points:

   The number of points charged in relation to the rate. In this case it's zero.

3. Lender fees:

The total fees charged that are retained by the lender or broker. These fees are not subject to change.

4. Third-party fees:

The total fees charged by parties other than your lender that are associated with completing your loan. These fees are typically estimated, since they may change, but they should never waver by more than plus or minus 10 percent. While it's rare, there are lenders that will guarantee these costs. Price guarantees are covered later.

At a 6 percent interest rate, your total cost is the sum of items two through four, for a total of $3,415. Simple, isn't it?

This MYOM Rate Sheet Quote requires the lender to add all of the costs considered lender fees and all the costs considered third-party fees and present each as one number. You will discover these costs remain constant regardless of the interest rate or points associated with the loan.

These costs are entered on the MYOM Quote Detail form. The portion of the form that is relevant at this point in our exercise appears on the next page (certain fields have been left intentionally blank).

The MYOM Quote Detail form includes all the fees you will encounter and includes spaces for fees and costs not named on the form. While the details are nice to know, what matters is the total cost in each column. Look at the total lender fees and total third-party fees on this form and you will see they are carried to their respective columns on the MYOM Rate Sheet Quote form.

There are other costs and settlement charges that are associated with a mortgage loan, but these costs have no bearing on price and are not subject to change among mortgage providers. The complete

MYOM Quote Detail form incorporates these costs, and they are explained later in chapter 11. (The complete form can be viewed in the appendices at www.mindyourownmortgage.com.)

Mind Your Own Mortgage
Quote Detail
www.mindyourownmortgage.com

Quote Date		Loan Type	Conventional
Loan Amount	$ 300,000	Loan Term	30 years
Lender		Amortization	Fixed
Contact Name		Escrow/Impounds	None
Contact Tel		Lock Term	30 days
Contact E-mail		Cash out?	No

Interest Rate	Lender Fees (Paid to Lender)	Third Party Fees (Paid to Others)
Payable in connection with the loan:		
Loan origination charges	$ 1,950	
Appraisal fee		$ 395
Credit report		$ 35
Tax Service		$ 40
Flood certification		$ 45
Other (describe) _____		
Other (describe) _____		
Other (describe) _____		
Title charges:		
Title services		$ 225
Settlement or closing fee		$ 350
Owner's title insurance		
Lender's title insurance		$ 375
Other (describe)		
Other (describe)		

Totals to MYOM Rate Quote Sheet:

	Lender Fees	Third Party Fees
Total Lender Fees	$ 1,950	
Total Third Party Fees		$ 1,465

INSIDER VIEWPOINT:

New Rules Force Lenders to Bundle Junk Fees

In November 2008, the US Department of Housing and Urban Development published new rules that included sweeping changes to the disclosures related to the mortgage quote and real estate settlement process. Two of these important changes were the elimination of junk fees and modifications to the related disclosures in the new Good Faith Estimate.

The total lender fees in our example amount to $1,950 and are quoted as one number. Prior to the new rules, lenders were able to unbundle their fees into several categories. The most typical fees included application fees, loan origination fees, processing fees, underwriting fees, document preparation fees, and wire transfer fees.

While the bundling of these fees into one number does not eliminate the existence of junk fees, it does provide the consumer value: using one number makes the total of the previously unbundled fees painfully apparent. In theory, this should drive down the cost of lender fees to consumers, since there isn't anywhere to stick small fees that can add up.

The bundling of junk fees also serves as verification of the MYOM Shopping System's premise: to arrive at one total for any given rate.

While the new ruling isn't a complete solution and does not provide the simplicity of the MYOM Shopping System, it is a big step in the right direction.

The Complete MYOM Rate Sheet Quote

Now that we've covered the basics, let's take a look at a completed MYOM Rate Sheet Quote using our assumptions. This is a critical step in the process of understanding of price and how the MYOM Shopping System can protect you from price manipulation, so pay careful attention as you read on.

The completed MYOM Rate Sheet Quote for our example follows:

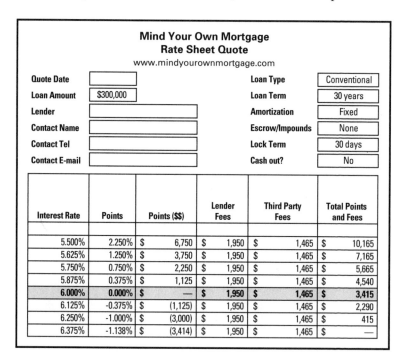

Mind Your Own Mortgage
Rate Sheet Quote
www.mindyourownmortgage.com

Quote Date		Loan Type	Conventional
Loan Amount	$300,000	Loan Term	30 years
Lender		Amortization	Fixed
Contact Name		Escrow/Impounds	None
Contact Tel		Lock Term	30 days
Contact E-mail		Cash out?	No

Interest Rate	Points	Points ($$)	Lender Fees	Third Party Fees	Total Points and Fees
5.500%	2.250%	$ 6,750	$ 1,950	$ 1,465	$ 10,165
5.625%	1.250%	$ 3,750	$ 1,950	$ 1,465	$ 7,165
5.750%	0.750%	$ 2,250	$ 1,950	$ 1,465	$ 5,665
5.875%	0.375%	$ 1,125	$ 1,950	$ 1,465	$ 4,540
6.000%	0.000%	$ —	$ 1,950	$ 1,465	$ 3,415
6.125%	-0.375%	$ (1,125)	$ 1,950	$ 1,465	$ 2,290
6.250%	-1.000%	$ (3,000)	$ 1,950	$ 1,465	$ 415
6.375%	-1.138%	$ (3,414)	$ 1,950	$ 1,465	$ —

The first and most important feature of the sheet to observe is this: it supplies the *entire* array of interest rate choices available for the loan being shopped. This information is essential to the shopping process, is largely ignored by the mortgage industry, and is not required by law.

There are a number of important observations to make about the Rate Sheet Quote:

Points are merely a function of the interest rate.

Points are the most commonly misunderstood element of a mortgage quote. Points are expressed as a percentage of the loan amount and, assuming the lender is priced fairly, are merely an adjustment to ensure the same profit margin to the lender, regardless of which rate you choose.

Study the relationship of points to the interest rate in the completed MYOM form: points are charged as the rate decreases and negative points (known as a rebate) are allowed as the rate increases. The retail par rate (or *zero-point rate*) is based on a target profit margin. Lower rates sell for less margin, so the lender charges points to make up the difference. The inverse is true as the rate increases, therefore the lender will provide a rebate (or negative points). The lender who is priced fairly will normally realize a constant profit regardless of the rate/point combination. This means the lender should be indifferent as to which interest rate you choose.

The standard increment for each interest-rate option is one-eighth of one point; however, the amount of points charged or rebate allowed will not behave in a linear fashion. The change in points from one rate to another is dependent on complex and changing market conditions that are beyond the scope of this text (and, fortunately, irrelevant to your quest to find the best price among several mortgage providers).

> *It is important to note that the rate and points are the only changing variables on the quote sheet.*

It is important to note that the rate and points are the *only* changing variables on the quote sheet.

Lender fees are constant.

Lenders charge certain fees for the service of providing the loan. These fees provide revenue in addition to the profit margin on the interest rate. The total is constant across the entire spectrum of the rate sheet. This should be the case with any price quote, since lender fees are the same regardless of what the rate/point combination is.

Third-party fees are constant.

While these fees are estimated, they are routine charges, and they can be provided with a close degree of accuracy by your lender. Once estimated, they can be added together and presented as one number, as we have done with the MYOM Quote Detail form. Notice that they are constant across the entire rate sheet, just like the lender fees.

Rate and total cost.

For each rate option, there is a total cost, which represents the sum of the points, lender fees, and third-party fees. Since lender and third-party fees are constant, the variation in total cost is entirely attributable to the interest rate. Rate and total cost are the two variables you will use to compare price among several lenders.

Note that the highest rate in our example carries no associated fees. This is known as the "no cost/no fee" loan. It is typically marketed as something proprietary and of no cost to you. However, it isn't proprietary and it certainly isn't free—you are paying for the lender and third-party fees in the form of a higher interest rate.

INSIDER TIP:
Getting the Information You Need

Mortgage brokers and certain lenders will commonly charge one point for their lender fee. This is often a source of confusion. When used in analysis of price, this "point" is not to be confused with points charged against the interest rate.

Many independent mortgage brokers and lenders who employ loan officers who set their own price don't maintain a retail rate sheet. This is because they set price on the fly, knowing what the margins are and pricing to what they can get away with. This is one of the primary reasons consumers are at great disadvantage.

You might run into situations where a mortgage salesperson does not know (or claims not to know) how to complete the MYOM Rate Sheet Quote form. In yet other situations, the lender may simply refuse or claim the information isn't available. (I have experienced this while posing as a shopper with both independent mortgage brokers and nationally known lenders.) In all such situations you should simply walk away. If the lender isn't going to be transparent with you, why conduct business with him?

As you use the MYOM Shopping System, you'll notice who argues against completing the forms and who doesn't; consequently, you'll be able to discern who's dealing straight and who isn't.

It's a Gallon of Gas

It took some time to get there, but the end result is simplicity. Here's your quote at the zero-point rate:

Loan Amount	Term/Type	Rate	Total Fees
$300,000	30-Year Fixed	6%	$3,415

It all comes down to two numbers: rate and total fees. The end result is no more complicated than a gallon of gas!

10

PRICE MANIPULATION

Janet: She's Out $2,500

Janet is a single mom. She holds a good job and can afford to make her payments, which is a relief, considering the demands of being the sole breadwinner in addition to being a single parent. She's got her wits about her and is her children's hero. She's sacrificing so they can go to college someday. Every penny counts in her household to this end.

Janet just refinanced her mortgage, after being contacted by a mortgage lender referred to her by a friend. The $2,500 payment on her mortgage was reduced and the interest rate was better, so she felt great about making the decision. Unbeknownst to her, the commissioned salesperson on the other end of the line stuck her with an additional percentage point in fees along the way. It was easy for him to do, since Janet innocently took the payment/rate bait—hook, line, and sinker.

With ten years left until her firstborn goes away to college, another $2,500 contribution to the college fund would have been substantial. But instead, it's locked up in her mortgage as a silent thief, racking up interest until the last payment she'll make on her mortgage—more than $12,000 when it's all said and done.

Janet's out $2,500. Wait just a minute—make that $14,500!

It happens all the time: price manipulation is a very common practice. In many lenders' minds, it's not manipulative to refrain from disclosing the entire rate sheet, but as you will see, not doing so allows the lender to squeeze additional profits at your expense without being caught in the act. Until now.

The MYOM Rate Sheet Quote requires lenders to communicate with you in their own language by forcing them to reveal the entire price picture for any loan. It is only through a review of all the rate options for a particular loan that you'll discover how lenders price their loans and thus be better able to protect yourself from being overcharged.

For a common example of price manipulation, let's suppose you are working with a commissioned salesperson who controls pricing. Assume his rate sheet looks exactly like the one used in our previous example (see the next page.) It's quite easy for him to slip in extra charges. Assume he quotes you 5.875 percent with three-quarters of a point. Study the quote sheet and you'll see the overcharge. It's going to be very difficult (if not impossible) to catch this without the MYOM form. The payment will be the same despite the additional charge because the loan amount doesn't change (there it is again: buying on payment is what causes so much trouble). This very common mistake will cost the consumer $1,125 in our example. Isn't it

Mind Your Own Mortgage
Rate Sheet Quote
www.mindyourownmortgage.com

Quote Date		Loan Type	Conventional
Loan Amount	$300,000	Loan Term	30 years
Lender		Amortization	Fixed
Contact Name		Escrow/Impounds	None
Contact Tel		Lock Term	30 days
Contact E-mail		Cash out?	No

Interest Rate	Points	Points ($$)	Lender Fees	Third Party Fees	Total Points and Fees
5.500%	2.250%	$ 6,750	$ 1,950	$ 1,465	$ 10,165
5.625%	1.250%	$ 3,750	$ 1,950	$ 1,465	$ 7,165
5.750%	0.750%	$ 2,250	$ 1,950	$ 1,465	$ 5,665
5.875%	0.375%	$ 1,125	$ 1,950	$ 1,465	$ 4,540
6.000%	0.000%	$ —	$ 1,950	$ 1,465	$ 3,415
6.125%	-0.375%	$ (1,125)	$ 1,950	$ 1,465	$ 2,290
6.250%	-1.000%	$ (3,000)	$ 1,950	$ 1,465	$ 415
6.375%	-1.138%	$ (3,414)	$ 1,950	$ 1,465	$ —

worth your time to obtain a proper quote in order to save $1,125 of your hard-earned cash?

To make matters worse, this $1,125 will haunt you to the very last payment you make on your loan, and it will transfer to all subsequent refinances. That's because it's now financed in the loan amount and each additional dollar borrowed is the last dollar paid off. Who knows, this additional charge could follow you for fifty years, racking up compounded interest all the while.

Isn't it worth your time to obtain a proper quote in order to save $1,125 of your hard-earned cash?

Suppose your current interest rate is 7 percent and you obtain a no cost/no fee quote of 6.50 percent. Since the rate is lower than you are paying now, on the surface it seems like a great deal. But what if the lender's internal rate sheet looks like the example we've studied? Your rate should have been 6.375 percent and you were stuck with an up-charge to the rate.

A professional salesperson can catch your weak spot and capitalize on it. Are you concerned about the rate? Perhaps you just want to lower it. Or maybe you're simply focused on lowering your payment. If your focus is this narrow, you are easy pickings for the salesperson!

Can you see how obtaining the entire rate sheet protects you? If you don't obtain one, your lender can play with the rate, points, and lender fees by moving the numbers around to a combination that is acceptable to you—and you won't have a clue about being overcharged.

Price manipulation is rooted in the fact that most consumers focus on the payment. This increases the ability of a lender to take advantage of borrowers and occurs with startling frequency in the retail mortgage business. When you use the MYOM Shopping System, you eliminate the ability of the lender to adjust price as he sees fit when moving from rate to rate.

11

Rate Locks and Other Important Price Details

Rod and Kathy: Playing the Market

Rod and Kathy started the refinance process about a month ago. The pitch made all the sense in the world—the broker quoted a mortgage rate and promised to give Rod a lower rate if rates decreased. The broker promised to keep an eye on the market so the loan could be locked at just the right time. He gave several reasons why he thought rates would most likely decrease over the ensuing weeks.

About thirty days into the process, the mortgage broker called with a sense of urgency. Rates were climbing and it was time to lock things in. Rod was initially upset, but after he checked out a few other places, he found rates had indeed climbed. After discovering his payment wasn't going to increase by much, he forgot all about it and closed the loan.

Rod and Kathy played the market and lost. The gamble resulted in their rate climbing from 5.5 percent to 5.75 percent and the mortgage broker pocketed a nice profit—despite having gambled with someone else's money. Imagine what would have happened if Rod objected by asking the broker to split the difference should interest rates rise. That would have been a good test of the broker's conviction, making him put his money where his mouth is.

And had Rod shopped around, he would have found the same loan at 5.3875 percent, with roughly the same in closing costs, locked upfront. Rod never saw it coming because he fell for the interest-rate pitch after making sure he'd be able to reduce his payments.

If you stick to the aim of keeping things simple, your mortgage shopping dollars will go a long way. The more bells and whistles your mortgage has, the more you are susceptible to paying too much, both when your loan funds and for the years that you hold it.

In this chapter, we'll round out your understanding of how to use the MYOM Shopping System so you can ignore any pitch that might subject you to price manipulation.

No–Cash-Out Refinance

Certain guidelines apply to the amount of cash that can be returned to a borrower upon closing a mortgage loan. Generally speaking, the amount of cash is limited to the lesser of $2,000 or 2 percent of the loan amount.

Take another look at our example MYOM Rate Sheet Quote:

Mind Your Own Mortgage
Rate Sheet Quote
www.mindyourownmortgage.com

Quote Date		Loan Type	Conventional
Loan Amount	$300,000	Loan Term	30 years
Lender		Amortization	Fixed
Contact Name		Escrow/Impounds	None
Contact Tel		Lock Term	30 days
Contact E-mail		Cash out?	No

Interest Rate	Points	Points ($$)	Lender Fees	Third Party Fees	Total Points and Fees
5.500%	2.250%	$ 6,750	$ 1,950	$ 1,465	$ 10,165
5.625%	1.250%	$ 3,750	$ 1,950	$ 1,465	$ 7,165
5.750%	0.750%	$ 2,250	$ 1,950	$ 1,465	$ 5,665
5.875%	0.375%	$ 1,125	$ 1,950	$ 1,465	$ 4,540
6.000%	0.000%	$ —	$ 1,950	$ 1,465	$ 3,415
6.125%	-0.375%	$ (1,125)	$ 1,950	$ 1,465	$ 2,290
6.250%	-1.000%	$ (3,000)	$ 1,950	$ 1,465	$ 415
6.375%	-1.138%	$ (3,414)	$ 1,950	$ 1,465	$ —

Due to the inverse relationship between points and the interest rate, total points and fees differ for each rate option. This, coupled with other closing costs that are not associated with price, will result in a change to the loan amount at closing due to the cash-out limitation.

When shopping for a no–cash-out refinance, it is acceptable to review interest rate options using the *same loan amount,* even though the loan amount is subject to change. Estimating the change in the loan amount is a useless exercise, since it has no impact on price. Because points are expressed as a percentage of the loan amount, the *dollar amount* might change, but not the *percentage.*

Loans without par rates

There may be times when there isn't a zero-point rate. This is because interest rates are quoted in 1/8 percent intervals and the market may be priced in between one of these intervals. If you encounter this, there's no reason to be suspicious.

Rate locks

Mortgage loans are priced to markets that can change on a daily or intraday basis. For this reason, your lender will offer the option to lock in your rate or float it until sometime later in the underwriting process. Rate locks are normally offered over ten-, thirty-, forty-five-, sixty- and sometimes ninety-day periods. The rate-lock term affects the price of your mortgage—the longer the lock period, the higher the cost of the mortgage (which becomes embedded in the price, usually in the form of an addition to points).

The cost of the lock will normally be charged prior to closing (once you have been approved for the loan) for lock periods exceeding forty-five days. These periods are most commonly with home buying and the reason for the up-front charge is associated with the cost to the lender of providing rate certainty and the likelihood that the borrower may switch providers if rates fall.

Any good lender can lock your loan upon completing a full application and obtaining an automated underwriting approval.

Any good lender can lock your loan upon completing a full application and obtaining an automated underwriting approval. As explained in chapter 8 this can be done in one sitting with the most sophisticated lenders. Therefore, assuming you qualify, you can lock your loan and get started as soon as you have determined who has the best price.

Alternatively, you will normally have the option of floating your rate. The selling feature is that you'll obtain a lower rate than the original quote if rates fall before your loan closes. There are several problems with this approach:

- The lender is gambling with your time and money.

  Because you haven't locked your loan, the lender has very little risk. If interest rates rise sharply, you may decide not to close your loan, but you are the one taking the risk. If rates decrease, it costs the lender nothing to look like a champ. Floating rates only serve to subject you to uncertainty because neither you nor the mortgage lender can predict interest rates.

- You lose price control.

  If you used the MYOM Shopping System and locked your rate, you know you still have the best price down the road. If you float your rate, you leave yourself wide open to price manipulation. Your original quote is now meaningless since rates change on a daily basis and the lender can pull the same price manipulation tricks outlined in chapter 10.

  You can't possibly follow mortgage interest rates from the time you apply to the time you lock in your rate. The lender uses tools that are not available to you in order to observe the market and adjust price. Even if you obtained them, the odds are long that you'd know how to use them. This allows your lender to squeeze a little more margin out of your loan without you knowing it.

- Lock and float.

  Some lenders offer a "free float down" option, allowing you

to lock in your rate and obtain the lower rate if rates fall. There is *no free lunch*! There is a cost to these types of programs.

I don't believe it makes sense to float your rate. It destroys price certainty, opens you up to price manipulation, and amounts to a gamble with your money while you lose control over the lender. Floating rates are like adjustable rate mortgages—they're full of risk. You should focus on obtaining the best price with the least chance of change. You will rest easy knowing you shopped wisely and locked in a rate you can count on.

INSIDER TIP:
The Ten-Day Rate-Lock Game

A lender may quote you a ten-day lock (with or without disclosing the lock term) in the hopes of luring you to the best price he can offer (the shorter the lock term, the better the price).

A ten-day rate lock simply means you must lock your rate no later than ten days prior to settlement. The problem with the price is that it *doesn't exist*, because you can't obtain it when it's quoted. Since it takes longer than ten days to close a loan, you can't obtain the ten-day rate until well after you have initiated the refinance process with the lender. Once you've spent your time and some money, it gets difficult to walk away, even if things go against your liking.

In order to sell the deal, the salesperson will extol the benefits of floating rates and promise to keep an eye on the market, so that you can time your lock. Again, he cannot predict interest

---

rate movements and neither can you. Don't fall into this trap!

A good lender will discuss rate locks with you, including the related rate-lock policies. Such a lender will objectively explain the rate lock options available to you and won't make claims about the market and which direction rates are headed. If you find a mortgage salesperson isn't objective about rate locks, be wary.

The rate-lock policy

Whenever you lock an interest rate, make sure you obtain the written rate-lock policy from the lender before committing your business.

If you are doing a refinance, you probably won't need an extension if you lock your loan for thirty to forty-five days, but you must be informed of the costs in case you do. If you are buying a home, delays can easily occur when buyers and sellers negotiate down to the wire. Lock-extension fees and terms vary greatly, so before you lock, make sure you read the lock policy and understand the costs, if any, associated with an extension.

Price guarantees

Although written price guarantees that cover lender and third-party fees are rare, you might run across a lender who will provide this. It doesn't hurt to ask.

At a minimum, there should be no change to the points and lender fees for any rate, as long as the assumptions used to obtain the quote remain valid. In addition, third-party fees should be estimated with very close accuracy; if they change down the road, your lender had better have a very good explanation.

INSIDER VIEWPOINT:
Price Guarantees

With the advent of automated underwriting, the narrowing of mortgage product options as a result of the credit meltdown, and because it is possible to estimate the impact of third-party fees with great accuracy, it is a shame price guarantees aren't commonplace. If you think about it, particularly with large lenders, there is a wealth of experience and data at their fingertips that could be used to drive guaranteed pricing.

Price guarantees were more commonplace in the early days of online lending. But as the Internet evolved, online lenders were acquired or exited the business, and price transparency died.

I have personal experience offering price guarantees on a nationwide basis. Extensive consumer research exists confirming the need for such pricing. After having funded billions in mortgage originations on a price guarantee basis, I have witnessed the value that price transparency, certainty, and simplicity bring to the marketplace and to the consumer.

Despite the constant push for greater transparency and certainty, price guarantees remain a rare commodity. I encourage you to seek lenders who are willing to put their money where their mouth is—by giving you a guarantee rather than just a Good Faith Estimate.

Escrows/Impounds

Assuming you have a choice, there is generally a price break applied to a loan when you use an escrow account to pay for property taxes and insurance. If you choose to use escrows, make sure the lender demonstrated the differential by showing you the price for the same loan without escrows/impounds.

Closing costs that have no bearing on the selection of a mortgage provider

Certain closing costs have no bearing on the selection of a mortgage provider because they will remain the same regardless of which lender you choose. These costs have been intentionally excluded from the MYOM Shopping System for the purpose of comparing price.

These costs include:

- Government recording fees and transfer charges.
- Prepaids and costs that will recur after the loan is closed (known by the industry as "recurring closing costs"). Examples include the initial deposit to be made to establish an escrow/impound account for the purpose of paying property taxes and insurance premiums; and prepaid interest, representing interest on your old loan from the beginning of the month to the date of the payoff and interest on your new loan from the date of the payoff to the end of the month.
- Settlement charges you can shop for, such as a home or pest inspection.

Prepaids are normally added to the principal balance of the new loan. The lender merely makes your new loan amount large enough to cover these costs. Although these costs are to be ignored for purposes of obtaining the price when shopping for a loan, they are included in the MYOM Quote Detail form for purposes of comparing them to the Good Faith Estimate, should you so desire. See the appendices at www.mindyourownmortgage.com for more information.

INSIDER TIP:
Pay for Prepaids and Impounds Out of Your Pocket

It's better to pay for prepaids and impounds out of your pocket than to roll them into your loan amount and finance them for the term of your new loan. Why? Because you normally pay for these without borrowed funds as part of the expense of owning your home. In the loan process, it's easy to roll these costs into the loan amount. The fix is simple: add the cost of the prepaids and impounds to your first mortgage payment and be done with it.

Things like home owner's insurance and property taxes shouldn't be financed because you'll end up paying interest on these borrowed funds for thirty years. Rolling your prepaid interest charges into the new loan may make it feel like you're skipping a payment, but you aren't. These costs are merely being borrowed at your new mortgage rate over the life of the mortgage.

Paying for something in cash that you'd incur anyway is sound financial practice. You'll save thousands of dollars in interest charges over the life of your mortgage by doing so.

The Real Estate Practices Act (RESPA) and the Good Faith Estimate (GFE)

In November 2008, the Department of Housing and Urban Development (HUD) issued new regulations under RESPA that took full effect in January 2010. The new regulations included many changes to existing law, which are aimed at bringing more transparency to the mortgage process and greater certainty for consumers.

RESPA is about closing costs and real estate–settlement procedures and requires that consumers receive disclosures at various times during the transaction. It also prohibits kickbacks to mortgage providers, making it illegal for a mortgage provider to pay any type of referral fee for business obtained, including any payments to prior customers.

Among the disclosure rights you have as a consumer is the right to obtain a GFE that details all loan closing costs and settlement charges *before you agree to move forward with the loan and/or pay any fees.* (The law does allow the lender to charge a fee for running a credit report, but you can find many lenders who won't charge you anything to take an application and run credit.) The law requires lenders to provide borrowers with a GFE within three days of the mortgage application date.

> **Among the disclosure rights you have as a consumer is the right to obtain a GFE that details all loan closing costs and settlement charges.**

The MYOM Shopping System is based on obtaining quotes no later than the day after completing a full mortgage application. Since the law says the GFE must be provided within three days of taking the application, you can demand the GFE be supplied along with the MYOM quote forms.

INSIDER TIP:
Use the Same Interest Rate for Each GFE

The GFE is only required in relation to a quote for a chosen interest rate, not for each rate option shown on the MYOM Rate Sheet Quote. While the GFE doesn't provide the consumer with a view of all interest-rate options for a given loan, it is nonetheless a valuable form.

In your shopping efforts, make sure you request a GFE for the *same interest rate* for each lender shopped. This places each GFE on equal grounds and will be useful when comparing quotes (see chapter 12).

Remember that the *only* fee that will change for any given interest rate is the points. This means all other price and closing-cost information on the MYOM forms and the GFE should agree for any rate option, while the rate and points will agree to only one of the rate options on the MYOM Rate Sheet Quote. See the appendices at www.mindyourownmortgage.com for an explanation of how to compare the GFE to the MYOM quote forms.

Points, lender fees, and third-party fees included in the MYOM Rate Sheet Quote form and the MYOM Quote Detail form were designed to match the definitions of tolerances in the HUD regulation, therefore making it possible to rely on written law in using the information contained in the shopping system forms.

By law, you have a right to be informed of the total cost of your loan. Accordingly, it can be inferred that you have a right to obtain information regarding price across the spectrum of interest-rate options in the manner provided by the MYOM Shopping System forms. This doesn't imply the MYOM Rate Sheet Quote must be completed by way of legislative instruction, but it does imply that it is reasonable to request the information contained in the forms as part of your right to obtain information about the total cost of your loan.

The new regulations also provide for certain tolerances as to the amount by which items included on the GFE can change. This is covered in chapter 14.

> *By law, you have a right to be informed of the total cost of your loan. Accordingly, it can be inferred that you have a right to obtain information regarding price across the spectrum of interest-rate options.*

INSIDER VIEWPOINT:
Good Faith Estimates Under the RESPA

The GFE provided for under RESPA's revised regulations is a big step forward in providing transparency and certainty to consumers in a mortgage transaction. However, the GFE falls short in the following ways:

- The GFE does not protect the consumer from price manipulation because it depends on only one rate point, given by way of the lender's quote. The consumer remains exposed to overcharges due to the narrow focus of the GFE.
- The GFE mixes apples and oranges by including fees related to price and costs that have no bearing on the selection of a mortgage provider; these all appear together as total settlement charges. This can lead to inaccurate price comparisons when using the shopping chart included on the GFE form.

The GFE is a decent tool, but it must be supplemented if you wish to protect yourself with a complete, accurate comparison of price quotes among several lenders.

The MYOM Shopping System solves this problem by helping you focus on price, separating it from costs that have no bearing on your selection of a mortgage provider. The MYOM Rate Sheet Quote helps to curb price manipulation because it forces the lender to disclose all interest-rate options for any particular loan, while the MYOM Quote Detail form allows you to ensure that lender fees and third-party fees remain constant across the spectrum of interest rate options.

A summary of how each section of the GFE relates to the MYOM Rate Sheet Quote and Quote Detail forms is included in the appendices at www.mindyourownmortgage.com.

Moving On

We have almost completed the MYOM Rate Sheet Quote. All we need to do is include the payment for each rate option—then we can examine how to compare offers.

12

It's Not About the Payment!

John's Payments

John is used to making his payments—two cars, his credit cards, and his mortgage. He doesn't think about the increase in his credit card bill, since the minimum payment isn't a big deal. He's got cash left over at the end of the month, so things are going well. Never mind the fact he's upside down when you factor the increase in his credit card balance from month to month.

When his broker called on him to refinance, John was offered a great loan that would save him $400 per month. He was able to take out some cash to pay down his credit cards and the extra $400 per month came in handy. John appreciated the personal service and care the broker took to get the job done.

In John's financial life, like many others', it's all about the payment. Not long after refinancing, John was able to trade in his older car for a new four-wheel-drive truck—complete with some off-road upgrades (although there isn't a dirt road within one hundred miles of John's house). John never thinks about the total long-run cost of all the payments he's making; all he sees is what he has and what the payments are. John's an easy sell for a mortgage pro, since he's been desensitized. Price never enters the picture. John's life is money in the broker's pockets—the broker can count on calling on him to refinance every three years or so. She'll give him the same great care to get the job done and lower his payments; plus she'll most likely earn another referral (financial birds of the same feather flock together). John's financial life offers an annuity to the mortgage broker when you combine the fifty or so relationships she has with people just like John.

John's mortgage payment means big money for his broker at the cost of John's financial future.

Shopping for a mortgage is about *price*, not about *payment*. What matters are the interest rate for the type of loan you choose and the total points and fees—*nothing else*.

Payment affordability must never come before price, lest you end up with a loan that will cause you grief. Affordability must be measured within the parameters of sound financial living (refer to chapter 5), instead of what you can qualify for.

Shopping for a payment will only lead to overcharges and mortgage woes.

The Complete MYOM Rate Sheet Quote

For the reasons discussed above, I've left the payment as the last step in building a complete rate sheet quote using our example mortgage assumptions. This completes the picture for the quote and allows you to step back and review your various options. The completed sheet looks like this:

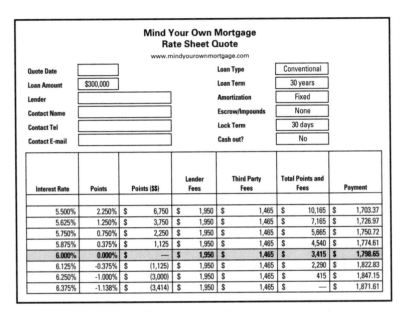

Mind Your Own Mortgage
Rate Sheet Quote
www.mindyourownmortgage.com

Quote Date		Loan Type	Conventional
Loan Amount	$300,000	Loan Term	30 years
Lender		Amortization	Fixed
Contact Name		Escrow/Impounds	None
Contact Tel		Lock Term	30 days
Contact E-mail		Cash out?	No

Interest Rate	Points	Points ($$)	Lender Fees	Third Party Fees	Total Points and Fees	Payment
5.500%	2.250%	$ 6,750	$ 1,950	$ 1,465	$ 10,165	$ 1,703.37
5.625%	1.250%	$ 3,750	$ 1,950	$ 1,465	$ 7,165	$ 1,726.97
5.750%	0.750%	$ 2,250	$ 1,950	$ 1,465	$ 5,665	$ 1,750.72
5.875%	0.375%	$ 1,125	$ 1,950	$ 1,465	$ 4,540	$ 1,774.61
6.000%	0.000%	$ —	$ 1,950	$ 1,465	$ 3,415	$ 1,798.65
6.125%	-0.375%	$ (1,125)	$ 1,950	$ 1,465	$ 2,290	$ 1,822.83
6.250%	-1.000%	$ (3,000)	$ 1,950	$ 1,465	$ 415	$ 1,847.15
6.375%	-1.138%	$ (3,414)	$ 1,950	$ 1,465	$ —	$ 1,871.61

The first thing you'll notice is the range of payments, from a high of $1,871.61 to a low of $1,703.37. This is normal and has to do with how the marketplace determines the adjustment to points relative to each rate option. But it presents a problem.

Assume you have shopped several lenders and decide to proceed with this quote. What rate and payment combination do you select? The answer doesn't lie in the payment; it lies in the interest rate and the total cost to obtain the rate. In other words, you need to think in terms of rate and *cost*, not rate and *payment*. Now the decision is rooted in how long it takes to recoup the cost associated with the rate.

For example, if you are buying a home and it's the last one you'll own, you'll recoup the $10,135 it costs to obtain the 5.5 percent rate.

171

But this isn't a realistic assumption. What if you end up having to move before you recoup the cost of your new mortgage?

If you consider a rate lower than 6.375 percent (there is no cost to obtain this rate), the trick is to calculate the number of months it takes to break even between this rate and any of the other choices. You can approximate the break-even point by taking the cost and dividing it by the difference in the payment. For example, the difference in total cost between the 6.375 percent and 6 percent rate is $3,415, and the difference in the corresponding payments is $73 per month. If you divide the difference in total cost ($3,415) by the difference in the monthly payments ($73) you arrive at 47. It therefore will take 47 months to break even if you choose the 6 percent rate, which means you must remain in the home for at least this long (without refinancing) before you begin to experience the benefits of the lower payment.

What if you are refinancing? If you have a fixed rate that is higher than 6.5 percent, it's a no-brainer to refinance to the 6.375 percent rate. This is because it costs you nothing out of your pocket to trade your current interest rate for the new one.

The Two-Year Rule

It's tempting to pay to buy down interest rates because of the difference in the payment. Personally, I make a rule to ensure any costs associated with obtaining a mortgage (except those which would be incurred anyway, such as prepaids) are recouped inside of two years. This rule applies to buying a home and refinancing your mortgage.

Here's another way to look at it: assume you were required to pay for all costs out of your pocket, rather than financing them in the loan amount. Would you be willing to shell out the cash in exchange for the lower payment? Probably not.

If this is the case, why would it be any different if you borrowed the money? It shouldn't be.

In a refinance, making the rate and cost decision is an *integral* part of the comprehensive refinance strategy. It doesn't stand alone and must be considered along with other factors in determining whether your refinance makes good economic sense. (We'll take a look at these factors in chapter 19.)

Let's get past the payment and move on. It's time to learn how to compare offers.

13

COMPARING OFFERS

Melissa: She Bought a Lower Interest Rate for $2,000

Melissa had studied the MYOM Shopping System. When she saw the time was right, she began to shop for a refinance. Rates had been declining, so she decided to see if she could lower the interest rate on her fixed-rate mortgage for an acceptable price.

After shopping several lenders, Melissa found three who were willing to complete the required forms. When it was all said and done, she had three quotes at the same interest rate for a new fixed-rate mortgage and the total cost for each. It was simple to decide who had the best deal. In the end, Melissa saved $750 over the next best quote and changed her interest rate from 5.75 percent to 5.25 percent for only $2,000. To ensure she'll save money and pay off her mortgage early, Melissa just keeps making the same payment on the new loan.

Melissa is well on her way to being mortgage free!

Once you've obtained your quotes, comparing them using the MYOM Shopping System is easy. Because you have obtained the right information, making a good decision is a snap.

Let's assume you've collected three quotes—now it's time to compare results and determine the best price. Presented below is a completed MYOM Quote Comparison form with our MYOM Rate Sheet Quote example from chapter 9 represented as Lender B:

Mind Your Mortgage
Quote Comparison
www.mindyourownmortgage.com

Loan Type	$ 300,000		Escrow/Impounds	None
Loan Term	30 years		Lock Term	30 days
Loan Type	Conventional		Cash out?	No
Amortization	Fixed			

Lender	Quote Date	Interest Rate	Points	Points ($$)	Lender Fees	Third Party Fees	Total Points and Fees
Lender A	1/15/01	6.000%	0.500%	$ 1,500	$ —	$ 1,525	$ 3,025
Lender B	1/15/01	6.000%	0.000%	$ —	$ 1,950	$ 1,465	$ 3,415
Lender C	1/15/01	6.000%	0.000%	$ —	$ 999	$ 1,475	$ 2,474

All of your quotes must be as of *the same business day, for the same loan, with the same terms.* Therefore, the loan information at the top of the form agrees with each MYOM Rate Sheet Quote.

Comparing quotes is a simple three-step process:

1. Select an interest rate—in this case, it's 6 percent.
2. Complete the MYOM Quote Comparison form (see the appendices at www.mindyourownmortgage.com):

- Enter the loan information at the top of the form.
- Enter the points, lender fees, and third-party fees from each MYOM Rate Sheet Quote for the chosen interest rate.
- Add the points, lender fees, and third-party fees together to arrive at the totals in the last column.

3. Pick a winner: the best price is the lender with the lowest total points and fees (in this case Lender C, who is priced $941 less than the highest quote).

It's that simple. Can you see how the MYOM Shopping System forces commodity-type pricing among lenders competing for your business? It levels the playing field, allowing you to make an objective decision.

You're in the driver's seat—and now it's as easy as picking which station at the intersection has the cheapest gallon of gas!

Some Revealing Observations

Study the rate quote comparison carefully and you'll notice Lender A has a worse deal but charges no lender fees. How can this be?

This phenomenon is one of the reasons the MYOM Shopping System is so powerful. Lenders commonly shift the numbers among categories that dictate profits, namely rate, points, and lender fees. This allows them to advertise lower prices in relation to only one element of price in order to lure potential customers to do business with them.

In this case, Lender A advertises that he doesn't charge a lender fee. This sounds appealing, and if you were focused only on this value proposition or the payment and didn't use the MYOM Shopping System, you'd miss savings of almost $1,000!

This type of pricing situation is *very common* in the mortgage industry, so much so that you must take into question any lender who claims to be offering something different. Remember, the four elements of price are universal to *all mortgage loans.* (You'll learn more about gimmicks like this in chapter 15.)

Take a look at the third-party fees and you'll notice the highest and lowest are only $50 apart. As a rule of thumb, third-party fees included in the MYOM Rate Sheet Quote should not vary by more than 10 percent from lender to lender. If you come across a lender with third-party fees that are considerably lower than your other quotes, examine the MYOM Quote Detail and determine the source(s) of the difference. Ask the lender to explain why his third-party fees are so much lower. If this lender has the best quote and you are considering doing business with him, I suggest asking him to put his money where his mouth is and obtain a written guarantee for the fees; if he balks, he is probably low-balling you.

What's Missing?

What's missing from the quote comparison sheet and the ensuing discussion? The mortgage payment!

This is intentional, so that you get the point: it isn't about the payment. To underscore this, consider this fact: the payment for each quote is exactly the *same.* That's right—$1,798.65 for each lender.

So why all the fuss? Why go through all this work if all the payments are the same? Because it's about price and not payment! And you bet there's some fuss—$941 worth, to be exact. That's the difference between the best and worst quote. Is that a lot of money to you? It is to me. Retaining $941 of cold, hard cash in your pocket should make it worth all the work it took to extract the information.

The costs to refinance your loan, unless you wish to pay them out of your pocket, will be added to your existing loan balance. This is accomplished by making the new loan just large enough to cover costs to refinance. Even with a no–cash-out refinance, some amount will be refunded to you at closing. In this example, the amount refunded at closing will be the difference between each quote.

Lender C's quote will yield $941 more cash at closing than Lender B's quote. Those are *real dollars* and *real savings*.

What's more, you can turn around and use the $941 to immediately pay extra on your mortgage after it is funded. Given the interest rate of 6 percent, this will save you $4,668 in interest charges over the life of the loan. When you look at it this way, Lender C's quote is $5,609 ($4,668 plus $941) better than the next best quote!

Are the lights shining brightly or at least flipped on now? Is it clear that you've been trained to think about the payment, which leads to bad decisions? Do not underestimate the importance of this lesson, because focusing on mortgage payments leads to more serious mistakes in managing your mortgage debt than any other issue.

A Note About Other Closing Costs

As discussed in chapter 9, government fees, prepaids, and nonrecurring closing costs have no bearing on your choice of a mortgage provider and are therefore omitted from the price comparison exercise. As a matter of fact, these costs should be exactly the same for all of your quotes, given that you have requested each quote with the same loan characteristics listed at the top of the MYOM Quote Detail form. This is because the nature of these costs and the circumstances that influence them do not change from one provider to the next. For example, you'll have to pay interest on your old loan to the date it is paid off and interest on your new loan from the date it is funded to the end of the month (this is referred to as prepaid interest).

Despite the fact these costs should be exactly the same, you'll find instances in which they're not. Here's a summary of the most common types of closing costs and the likelihood of differences (the terms used are the same as those found on a GFE):

• *Government transfer taxes*

Because government fees are published and standardized, there is little chance of a difference. If you find differences, it is most likely due to an omission on the part of the lender with the lower cost.

• *Government recording charges*

These may not be exactly known at the time of the quote, so these costs could change. In any event, the change should never be more than 10 percent from the original quote (thus, all of the quotes should be comparable within 10 percent of each other).

• *Prepaids/recurring closing costs*

1. Initial escrow deposit:

   Since the standards for an escrow should be the same for agency or government-sponsored loan programs, you should find no differences. If the loan is not associated with an agency or government program, differences may be due to variations in the escrow program. Make sure you inquire whenever you find a difference.

2. Prepaid interest:

   This represents interest on your old loan from the beginning of the month to the date of the payoff and interest on the new loan from the date of the payoff to the end of the month.

There is a high likelihood of differences in this charge, and it occurs when each lender assumes a different closing date scenario (for example, one lender may assume the loan will close in the middle of the month and another at the end of the month). This leads to a logical difference in the resulting interest calculations but continues to have no bearing on your choice of a provider.

• *Costs you can price shop for*

If you are buying a home, settlement charges you can shop for such as a home or pest inspection are subject to variation.

If you find large differences in any of these costs, you should ask the lenders who differ to explain them. The answer should always be due to an assumption that caused the difference (like the example regarding prepaid interest).

For a detailed list of these closing costs and how to reconcile the MYOM Quote Detail to the GFE, see the appendices at www.mindyourownmortgage.com.

Buying a Home

Tom and Katie: Emotionally Tied to the Purchase

Tom and Katie just fell in love with the home. It was perfect for them and their plans to raise a family. Ellen, their real estate agent, was kind, professional, and wise—she knew that Tom and Katie's emotions would allow her to control all aspects of the transaction.

Enter Ellen's mortgage broker. If they wanted to close on their home without any bumps, it would be wise to work with Ellen's team, she said. That made sense to Tom and Katie, so they never shopped the mortgage. Sixty days after their offer was accepted, Tom and Katie moved into their new home. Ellen left them a nice housewarming gift and a personal card thanking them for their business. She was just great!

Several months later, Katie was pregnant. Tom was a bit stressed about coming up with the money for the nursery, although he wanted to make the baby's room just as Katie wished. If only they had shopped for their mortgage, they would have saved more than $2,000 at closing—more than enough to cover the nursery expenses, and diapers for a few months too.

Alas, Tom and Katie became emotionally tied to the purchase and neglected to shop.

A refinance transaction was used to explain and demonstrate the MYOM Shopping System. The system can also be used for the home-buying process. The major differences are:

• *Price*

If you are buying a new home, it is common for the builder to offer a discount if you use his mortgage solution, but that does not mean you shouldn't shop around (it would be foolish not to, to at least to investigate the legitimacy of the discount being offered).

Third-party fees are normally limited, since the seller will pay for most of them, except the appraisal.

The interest rate, points, and lender fees behave in the same manner for a home purchase as they do for a refinance.

• *Rate locks*

Lock periods tend to be longer, due to the time to complete the sales transaction. As with a refinance, make sure you use the same lock terms for your quotes.

It is more likely that you will float your rate if the closing is more than forty-five days out, due to the cost of longer rate-lock periods. Obtain the cost of the rate lock and make a decision based upon the cost and your willingness to assume the risk of rising rates.

• *Services you can shop for*

Pest and home inspections are the major categories. As explained earlier, these have no bearing on your selection of a mortgage provider.

A word of caution is warranted: your real estate agent will normally prefer to use his mortgage provider. This is because the agent's commission is on the line and he wants a mortgage provider he is familiar with (and can push around if he has to).

If you are a highly qualified buyer and can remain unemotional about the home-buying process, I strongly suggest you shop around for your home-purchase mortgage before committing to a mortgage broker referred to you by the real estate agent (it is more common for real estate agents to work with brokers than with direct lenders, because of the personal business relationships real estate agents prefer to maintain). Most often, the person your real estate agent suggests will be a commissioned salesperson, which you now know comes with certain risks. The real estate agent is motivated by his commission as well, so naturally he's going to refer a mortgage professional that he's comfortable with.

Shop around and go for the best price, not for the comfort a real estate agent promises with the broker he has presented—remember, both are tied to their commissions.

If the real estate agent presses hard for his mortgage solution, be on high alert! Do not allow your agent to influence your decision to shop for the best mortgage at the best price. This is independent of the real estate agent's process; a professional, seasoned agent should not care about your choice of lenders.

14

FROM QUOTE TO CLOSING

Brett and Ellen: Raked Over the Coals

Brett and Ellen went for the refinance after speaking with one lender. They decided to lock their interest rate and felt secure going into the transaction.

During the loan application process, Brett and Ellen were a bit unrealistic in estimating their income. As they waded through the loan process, one thing after another popped up. Brett is self-employed and didn't have good records for his current year income; Ellen is in sales with one great year in the past three. These issues made circumstances much different than when the loan was quoted based on what they'd provided the lender. In addition, their home appraised for 10 percent less than they had anticipated.

When it came time to close the loan, Brett and Ellen were hit with significant additional charges. They hadn't shopped their loan, nor had they been prepared to ensure they completed an accurate mortgage application. Without the proper knowledge going in, they were moving forward with no basis of understanding about what could go wrong once the loan process started.

By the time it came to fund their loan, they felt invested in the process and went ahead with it, despite it costing far more than they had anticipated and providing little real economic benefit.

Brett and Ellen raked *themselves* over the coals.

Once you have selected a lender, the loan process begins. This entails many steps, the most important of which involve verification of information taken in the mortgage application and information concerning the property:

- Your income—which must be verified by supporting documentation.
- The value of your home—which must be determined by way of an independent appraisal.
- Your credit rating—which will be reviewed prior to closing to ensure there have been no significant changes.
- Certain assets—such as any required cash reserves, or the source of a down payment if you are buying a home, must be verified.
- Your debts—which will be verified to ensure the information used to calculate debt ratios is accurate.
- Title examination—to ensure there are no liens on your property that must be subordinated to the new loan or issues that would inhibit obtaining clear title.
- Demand—your lender will issue a payoff demand letter to

your current lender to verify the amount required to pay off your existing mortgage.

Potential Price Changes

Your mortgage quote is based upon the assumptions and information contained in the mortgage application and your credit report. When the information used to complete the mortgage loan application differs from what is discovered while the loan is being processed, your mortgage quote may be subject to change. These price changes are in standard amounts and will usually be limited to an adjustment to the points. The most common circumstances causing a price change follow:

- *Debt ratios*

  Differences due to the discovery of new debts or differences in the amount of income upon examination of your income documentation. As debt ratios increase, so will your price. The inverse is also true.

- *Loan to value*

  A difference in the appraised value in your home from the originally estimated value used at the time of the quote, thereby causing a difference in the ratio of the loan amount to the value of the home. As the LTV increases, so will your price. The inverse is also true.

- *Changes in your credit score*

  There are circumstances that might require a lender to have another look at your credit prior to closing. If there are significant changes, this could affect your price. As your credit deteriorates, so will your price. The inverse is also true.

• Floating rates

Your interest rate is subject to change until you lock your rate. As discussed earlier, it is best to lock your rate as soon as you select a lender (unless the lock period is unusually long, as sometimes is the case when you are purchasing a home).

• Lock expiration

If your interest rate expires because your loan does not close within the lock period, there may be an additional charge. You can determine this up front by ensuring you obtain a written rate-lock policy (along with disclosure of any charges for rate expiration and extensions) along with your quote.

• Difference in qualification

In extreme circumstances, if you have marginal credit or your income documentation is inadequate, you may discover you don't qualify for the loan that was quoted. You should be able to determine if this is likely to occur, however, based on how clean your mortgage application information is. You know your financial situation better than the lender does, so make sure you discuss any doubts you have about the information being provided during the application process.

In addition, your third-party fees may change. If your lender has not provided a guarantee, the total of these charges should not change by more than 10 percent.

Limiting the Risk of Price Changes

I've given you several things that can change the price, but it's not as bad as it may seem at first glance, nor does it lessen the importance of shopping for the best deal.

You can significantly limit the risk of price changes by being as accurate as possible with your mortgage-loan application. If you are unsure about the ability to document an income source, don't count on it—it's better to be accurate than to be surprised later. Make sure you give an accurate and complete accounting of all of your debts, including terms and payments.

If your income is easy to determine and is steady, your credit is clean, you are accurate about your debts, and you have a good handle on the value of your home, there is little chance of a change in price from the original quote. The cleaner your mortgage application data is, the more likely it is the assumptions used to calculate price will hold up.

Establishing the Baseline

You should view the original mortgage quote as a baseline: any changes in price (so long as you remain qualified for the loan you selected) will be made in reference to the baseline. This means they can be tracked. Assuming you have locked your rate, you can control the information flow so that you are informed of any change in price as it occurs. Not only should you demand this, you have a right by law to the information.

The Law Protects You

The new HUD/RESPA regulations, which took full effect in January 2010, provide for certain tolerances in price and closing costs from the date the GFE was given to the date the loan is settled. If there are no significant discoveries during the underwriting process that dictate a price change (as discussed above), the following tolerances apply:

- Interest rate. From the time the rate is locked, this cannot change.
- Points (expressed as a percentage of the loan amount). From the time the loan is locked, these cannot change.

In addition, regardless of discoveries that may cause a price change, the following applies:

- Lender fees. No tolerance—these cannot change under any circumstances.
- Third-party fees. These can change, but by no more than 10 percent higher or lower than the original estimate for the total of all costs.

If changed circumstances result in a change in rate or points, the lender must provide you with a new GFE within three business days of the discovery of the change. As suggested above, you must track changes in price from the baseline; the law enables you to do so.

When the lender supplies you with a new GFE, you must ensure you know exactly what has changed. You can easily cross-reference any change in your GFE to the MYOM Quote Detail by using the appendices at www.mindyourownmortgage.com.

HUD-1a and HUD-1 Settlement Statements

Upon settlement of your loan, the lender is required by federal law to provide you with a final statement of all charges and costs associated with your mortgage refinance or home purchase. The settlement statement is the final accounting for the transaction.

The HUD-1a is used for refinance transactions and the HUD-1 is used for a home purchase.

You are going to have a tough time dealing with any surprises *after* your loan closes, so you must take advantage of your rights *before*. Federal law *requires* lenders to provide the settlement statement one day prior to closing, *but only if you request it.*

This is an essential step that you must not overlook. Inform the lender in advance that you will require the HUD-1/1a to be delivered the day before you close. This will give you an opportunity to make sure the price elements listed on the HUD-1/1a agree to the original MYOM Quote

> *Federal law requires lenders to provide the settlement statement one day prior to closing,* **but only if you request it.**

Detail form. Comparing the HUD-1/1a to the MYOM Quote Detail form is easy, the HUD form includes reference numbers that match the reference numbers of the MYOM Quote Detail. (See the appendices at www.mindyourownmortgage.com).

Under federal law, any changes in price can only be associated with one or both of the following:

- Third-party fees may change, but by no more than 10 percent from the original quote.
- A change in the rate or points due to changed circumstances after the original quote, as described in this chapter.

This covers three of the four price elements: rate, points, and third-party fees. Lender fees cannot be changed under any circumstances.

If you find changes in price between the HUD-1 and the original mortgage quote, other than any change that occurred due to the two points listed above, put the brakes on the transaction and deal with it immediately; don't allow the loan to close without resolving the differences.

INSIDER TIP:
Documentation Supporting Price Changes

You have a legal right to information pertaining to the cost of your mortgage. If your rate or points change (or your third-party fees change by more than 10 percent), I suggest you ask for supplemental information that gives explicit explanation for any change. Don't accept a change without understanding why the change occurred. Take the position that you have the right to this detailed information—because you do.

As an example, you would typically experience a price change if your loan to value increases from 70 percent to 80 or your FICO score decreases from 740 to 700. Lenders maintain computerized or manual internal pricing matrixes that are used to determine your original price quote based upon your mortgage application and credit report data. Since these factors were used to price your loan at the onset, it stands to reason the lender would have documentation supporting any change in price due to a change in these factors.

Any price change should be represented by the standard charges associated with the change in the related price factor (such as your FICO score or the loan to value). These charges are set by the secondary market (Fannie Mae, Freddie Mac, and government loan programs such as the FHA)—not the lender. It is imperative, therefore, that you demand specific information from the lender's computer system or other hard copy internal evidence supporting the price change. Don't leave this to a verbal communication or a change that is only represented in a revised GFE.

Remember, mortgages are priced as a commodity through the entire distribution chain, except for the interface with the consumer. Price adjustments are changes to the commodity based on standard amounts. Don't pay more than you have to; demand a peek inside so you can view these commodity-based price changes firsthand.

15

GIMMICKS

Brent:
He Won't Sink to the Level of the Competition

Brent owns a mortgage company with a couple of other partners. They've developed quite a business over the years by providing up-front, straightforward advice to home owners.

Brent's company is advertising on a couple of radio stations against several competitors, two of which have come up with a new pitch that's making it difficult for Brent's company to compete. Interest rates are in the 5 percent range and his stiffest competitor advertises a free mortgage loan with the following radio pitch:

Have you felt ripped off by your mortgage lender, promised one thing and then getting another, getting stuck with surprise costs at the last second? Isn't it time someone deals you a straight deck of cards? Just call us and see if you qualify for our exclusive free mortgage program—no application fees, no closing costs, and nothing out of your pocket. That's right—we'll lower your interest rate, lower your payment, and

*put you into a new loan, and it won't cost you a dime at closing. Call us
today and find out if we can help you.*

Since this ad has been running, Brent has noticed a dramatic drop
in mortgage inquiries. He knows his competitor doesn't have anything different, so Brent mystery shops the "free mortgage," knowing
that it's simply a full-rebate loan (the highest rate on the lender's rate
sheet that allows enough profit to pay for the closing costs). After
digging in, he finds the lender's no-cost loan is a quarter of a percent higher than the market, but since rates only dropped recently,
enough home owners are responding to the call for the "free loan"
and lower payment to take the deal without shopping it.

Despite the temptation, Brent refuses to sink to the level of his
competition. So he fires an honest shot across the bow, explaining in a new radio ad that there's no such thing as a free lunch.
Everyone has a no-cost option and his company is no different. His
ad challenges borrowers to shop for their loan and take the best
deal—even if it isn't his.

Fortunately for his customers, Brent didn't make up some bogus
claim just to get his phone to ring. The new ad works, and Brent has
put the kibosh on his competition.

If you were selling footballs, how would you extract more for your
product than the next guy? You wouldn't be able to do much, unless
you got really creative. Maybe you could hire Peyton Manning to
stand behind your product. Or somehow make it the official ball of
the National Football League. Then your football would have a perceived—but essentially manufactured—difference from the rest.

In a market where there isn't much of a difference in the product from one provider to the next, differentiation must be manufactured. As you know, mortgages are made of money—and money is just money. There isn't a difference from one fixed-rate mortgage to the next, or between any other mortgage products for that matter.

Because lenders realize mortgages are a commodity, the industry *as a whole* protects profits by withholding simplicity in the price equation and capitalizing on the consumer's propensity to focus on the payment. The MYOM Shopping System solves this problem.

On an *individual basis*, lenders go a step further to concoct differentiation in an effort to get your attention so you'll call them first. Once they have you on the line, the clever ones know all too well they can capture the sale by doing what the industry does *as a whole*, appealing to the desire to lower payments and taking advantage of the lack of information that prevents consumers from comparing multiple quotes.

If you listen closely to advertisements (mostly aired over radio) or your loan officer, you will notice the sales pitch is focused on one or a combination of the following:

- The rate
- Reducing your monthly payment, "saving you hundreds of dollars per month"
- Closing costs

The trick is to attack your point of weakness by appealing to the payment and to use other gimmicks to sound different, despite the fact there aren't any differences.

Now that you've learned how to shop for price, you'll be able to see through the various claims lenders make in their advertisements. You'll notice regional and lesser-known lenders and mortgage brokers tend to make the most appealing claims (nationally recognized brand-name lenders don't want to risk a class action law suit). You'll immediately recognize gimmicks and falsehoods associated with claims of differentiation embedded in what we're about to cover.

We'll use the same pricing information used in the MYOM Rate Sheet Quote from chapter 9 to help expose the advertising gimmicks lenders use to lure you in. Assume the following represents the internal pricing of a local mortgage company:

ABC Mortgage
Internal Price Sheet

Loan Amount	$ 300,000		Escrow/Impounds	None	
Loan Term	30 years		Lock Term	30 days	
Loan Type	Conventional		Cash out?	No	
Amortization	Fixed				

Interest Rate	Points	Points ($$)	Lender Fees	Third-Party Fees	Total Points and Fees	Payment
4.990%	2.225%	$ 6,750	$ 1,950	$ 1,465	$ 10,165	$ 1,608.63
5.125%	1.250%	$ 3,750	$ 1,950	$ 1,465	$ 7,165	$ 1,633.46
5.250%	0.750%	$ 2,250	$ 1,950	$ 1,465	$ 5,665	$ 1,656.61
5.375%	0.375%	$ 1,125	$ 1,950	$ 1,465	$ 4,540	$ 1,679.91
5.500%	0.000%	$ —	$ 1,950	$ 1,465	$ 3,415	$ 1,703.37
5.675%	-0.375%	$ (1,125)	$ 1,950	$ 1,465	$ 2,290	$ 1,736.45
5.750%	-1.000%	$ (3,000)	$ 1,950	$ 1,465	$ 415	$ 1,750.72
5.875%	-1.138%	$ (3,415)	$ 1,950	$ 1,465	$ —	$ 1,774.61

The mortgage company will weave messaging to make it sound like they have something different, when all they are doing is focusing on a different part of the rate sheet. Using the numbered references on the sheet, here are some of the statements you might hear:

- *"Can you believe it? Rates for a thirty-year fixed-rate loan under 5 percent!"* (Reference 1)

Assume rates have been in the 6 percent range for some time and a drop in the market brings them to the mid-fives. This lender sets the lowest rate on the sheet to 4.99 percent and sends a message about rates under 5 percent. Along with this message will be a call to urgency, reminding you of the days when rates were at 6 percent.

The pitch starts with the rate but is focused on the payment after you call on the lender. This is a simple sale to the uninformed consumer: 4.99 percent (just a hair under 5 percent) and a payment lower than the one you already have.

- *"Our rates are under 5 percent and we can save you hundreds of dollars per month!"* (Reference 2)

Assume the same market conditions with a recent drop in rates. The pitch is slightly different because it places the focus on the payment. The lender knows the allure to lower payments is strong and they'll fish out all those who will bite.

- *"Listen carefully: if your rate is over 6 percent, you need to call us today!"* (Reference 3)

Assume the same market conditions. This is yet another rate-oriented play that is focused on those who have not taken action and are still holding mortgages in the 6 percent range. Same rate sheet, different message.

- *"We specialize in no-cost loans!"* or *"We are your no-cost lender!"* (Reference 4)

There is no specialty here. All lenders have a no-cost rate option, which is simply the highest rate for any particular loan program that generates a rebate high enough to cover lender and third-party fees. In this case, the lender is referring to the 5.875 percent rate without having to quote it in his ad.

This gimmick is used predominantly when rates have

increased and don't sound appealing to prospective borrowers. Instead of sending a rate or payment message, the lender sends a message about no-cost loans. After you call, the pitch will refer to a special no-cost loan program, uniquely available with this lender.

I don't know about you, but any company that makes exaggerated claims about its products and claims exclusivity to something that isn't exclusive isn't going to get my business. Now that you are knowledgeable, you ought to be offended (this one has always offended me).

- *"We don't charge lender fees!"* (Reference 5)

Although it isn't depicted on the rate sheet, this claim involves combining lender fees with points. In this case, $1,950 would be eliminated from the lender fees column and buried in the points column.

This message is most commonly used when rates have edged upward, so a gimmick founded in another price element is used to solicit interest. Now that you know this is nothing more than a slick advertising ploy, why call this lender?

The point of this exercise is obvious by now. In each case, the lender has simply set five hooks with different bait, hoping a fish is going to bite. It looks different on the outside, but what's inside is always the same.

Stop and Think

It is imperative you stop, take notice, and reflect on what you've learned:

- There is *no difference* in the loan product for any of these pitches, since they are all based on the same rate sheet, yet each message communicates something that sounds markedly different.
- The messages are focused on rate, payment, or cost, all of which are designed to remove your focus from price. The lender hopes you won't catch on.
- Priced honestly, the lender is indifferent to any rate you choose. Remember, points are merely an offset to the rate and should yield the lender the same amount of profit whether you select the highest rate on the sheet or the lowest.

> *You must not allow yourself to be drawn to messages about rate or payment, or you will make big mistakes in managing your mortgage debt!*

- The uninformed shopper who responds to these types of messages is susceptible to price manipulation and overcharges, since the entire rate sheet won't be disclosed and the sales pitch has diverted attention from what matters.
- Be wary of lenders who make such claims. They'll be less likely to cooperate when you unleash the MYOM shopping system.

You must not allow yourself to be drawn to messages about rate or payment, or you will make big mistakes in managing your mortgage debt! Instead, you must focus on price and, if you are refinancing, whether the refinance is a sound financial decision.

There Are No Differences

Now you understand how lenders can position their loan products, promoting various elements of price or the payment in an effort to create differentiation in a market where there isn't any.

The types of mortgage available have been significantly reduced with the advent of the credit crisis. This only serves to expose those who make exclusivity claims for what they are—nothing but hot air. Now that you have been educated, you'll see right through it.

INSIDER TIP:
Mortgage Brokers Aren't All That Different

As explained in chapter 3, mortgage brokers are intermediaries between the primary mortgage market (direct lenders) and the consumer. The only reason for their existence is the desire of primary mortgage market players to write additional mortgages. For example, a lender with no retail presence in California may wish to conduct business in the state. Rather than advertise directly to the consumer, this direct lender may engage in what is known as the wholesale business by obtaining loans through a broker.

Now that you understand a little more about the intermediary relationship, it becomes obvious brokers don't have access to anything different than the lenders do; hence, there isn't any market differentiation as to product or price, and any attempt to create one is based on falsehoods.

Mortgage brokers will commonly claim differentiation based

on the value of the personal relationship. Since the MYOM Shopping System forces commodity-type price presentation, allowing you to make an objective decision, what's the use of a personal relationship?

About the only differentiation a mortgage broker provides is product breadth under one roof (which can be at the expense of price). A small broker that's been in the business for a long time develops a solid knowledge of mortgage products and, if it's approved with the right lenders, will have access to a wide range of products. Large lenders, on the other hand, typically focus on volume and will often have narrower product offerings (yet better prices).

If you stick with plain-vanilla fixed-rate mortgages, you'll find very little benefit to working with a broker versus directly with the lender.

Some Other Gimmicks

Most claims made by lenders are market driven. That is, they will focus on a certain portion of the rate sheet, depending on the level of interest rates. Low interest-rate environments will bring pitches related to rates and lower payments, while higher interest-rate environments will bring messages related to closing costs or fixed-rate messages aimed at people who are exposed to increasing rates (such as those holding ARMs).

There are other claims that have nothing to do with market conditions, yet are made with the same purpose in mind: to get you to believe they have something different (or at least interesting) so you will call them. Here are two common examples:

"We shop all the lenders, finding you the best rates."

Mortgage brokers will commonly exaggerate the value of shopping your mortgage among several lenders.

First, brokers cannot shop all of the lenders, because a broker must be approved by a lender in order to do business with him. The market isn't set up as an open exchange in which any broker with a complete mortgage application can walk up to a lender's window and request a quote. It's nearly impossible for a mortgage broker to do business with more than a half dozen lenders because each lender does business a little differently. Finally, brokers do better business-wise when they develop relationships and mortgage-application volume with one or two lenders.

"No payments until October."

Let's say it's early August, and you are looking to refinance your mortgage. The salesperson tells you it's a great time because he can fund your loan by September and you won't have to make any payments until November. You'll get to skip a payment!

This is nothing more than a sales gimmick and a lie. You will *never* skip a payment on your mortgage—the only time you won't have a payment is when you've paid it off.

Here's the truth: if your loan closes on September 15, you will pay interest on your old loan for the first fifteen days of September and interest on your new loan from the sixteenth to the end of the month. This brings your new loan paid to October 1, with your first payment due on November 1 for October interest. (Mortgage interest is always paid in arrears.) Notice that you have still paid interest for a thirty-day period. This is normally added to your new loan balance, which enables the illusion you are skipping a payment. You are paying for this whether it's out of your pocket (which is my recommendation) or whether you financed it.

⸻

Believe me, if you've been around the mortgage business for as long as I have, you've heard every trick in the book to get you to call and commit to a lender. Any claim that sounds like it's under market or a great deal is a gimmick. It stands to reason that the more outrageous the claims tend to be, the more unlikely the lender is to cooperate when you attempt to take control by using the MYOM Shopping System. The manner in which he has advertised his product should tip you

> *Any claim that sounds like it's under market or a great deal is a gimmick.*

off he is much more likely to manipulate price in an effort to get you to focus on something less than the entire picture. This should make you wonder whether he'll be straight with you.

My advice is to stay away from lenders making claims that sound too good to be true or those that emphasize selling points that detract from your attempt to collect the information you need. A lender should earn your business based solely on a fair price after you have shopped and compared. Don't let anything else enter into your decision.

Remember that old adage—if it sounds too good to be true, it probably is. I recall one percent mortgage rates being advertised on the radio prior to the meltdown. These were "option ARM" or "pick a payment" loans with a one percent rate that was good for one month. Need I say more?

INSIDER VIEWPOINT:
The Most Outrageous Gimmick I've Ever Seen

The lengths lenders and brokers will go to adopt false (or at least exaggerated) messaging as market conditions change astounds me. The most outrageous I've witnessed occurred in 2007–2008, when interest rates were in the mid-6 percent range. At the time, there were several companies advertising rates at 4.5 percent. They also claimed their customers would receive thousands of dollars a year from them just for refinancing to the 4.5 percent loan.

At the time, a note rate below 5 percent was an impossibility (the note rate is the rate written on the mortgage). After extensive research, I found the sad truth about the 4.5 percent loan program. Here's how it went down:

- The broker was writing note rates at 7.25 percent (give or take, depending on the market). This was the rate at the full rebate price—the no-cost loan.
- Assuming a $400,000 loan, the lender was priced to earn about 3 percent, which amounts to $12,000.
- The broker would return enough money (about $4,500 in this case) to the borrower to effectively "reduce" their rate to 4.5 percent for four to five months. The broker positioned this as if he were sharing his profit with the borrower.
- After four months, the broker would have the borrower

apply once again, writing yet another mortgage at the no-cost, no-fee rate and returning the difference.

I mystery shopped the 4.5 percent gimmick, and a salesperson attempted to convince me it was worth giving up my 5.5 percent fixed-rate for this scam. I was appalled at the number of consumers who fell for this gimmick. There are a number of problems with this product:

- Investors/Mortgage-loan servicers expect, on average, loans to remain on the books for five to seven years. This is a major factor driving the price paid for the mortgage. Loans must generally stay on the books for 120 days, or the broker will be required to return the amount he was paid. This scam essentially amounted to fraud against the investor/servicer, since the broker had full intent to refinance the loan as soon as he could get away with it and keep his profits.
- Consumers refinancing out of a lower fixed-rate were taking great risk. Should their property values have declined, they would not be able to refinance and would be stuck with the 7.25 percent note rate.
- The mortgage broker wasn't sharing much profit with his customers, since he was jacking up his no-cost rates. The gimmick was strong enough to hook many borrowers before they had a chance to shop. Funny thing (actually not funny) is a lot of the money returned to the customer

was the customer's money (not the broker's profit), since the rate was so high.

Fortunately for the brokers offering this shameful product, interest rates declined enough to offer a valid 4.5 percent note rate, but not without stiff fees to buy down the rate. I shudder to think how many consumers who fell for this gimmick ended up coming back and paying through the nose to obtain a fixed rate they could live with.

Shopping Summary

Hopefully, the discussion on price and how to compare offers has enlightened you and motivated you to ensure you obtain the right information before you obtain your next mortgage loan. As a summary, remember the following when shopping:

- Keep it simple—I like to stay with a fixed-rate loan, which makes it easy for me to understand what I'm getting into and gives me the security and certainty that my mortgage payments won't change.
- Know the big three—credit score, income, and the estimated value of your home.
- It's not personal, it's just business. You are shopping for a pile of money—make it all about price and ignore the salesperson's attempt to personalize the transaction.
- Use the MYOM Rate Sheet Quote to obtain a complete

quote from at least three lenders on the same day. All the quotes need to be for the same type of loan and terms.

- Complete a full mortgage application with each lender. Remember, you don't have to pay a dime to obtain the quote. If the lender wants to charge you anything, forget it and move on.

- For each rate for a particular loan, there are points, lender fees, and third-party fees. All other costs, including prepaids, are irrelevant to your selection of a mortgage provider.

- Review the quotes for reasonableness, ensuring you've obtained a MYOM Quote Detail form from each lender.

- Compare offers by selecting the same rate for each lender and determine the total cost for each. The lender with the best price will have the loan with the lowest total fees for the selected rate.

- If you meet resistance while shopping, don't back down. If a lender doesn't cooperate or insists upon selling to you without disclosing the full range of price using the MYOM forms, *walk away*.

- Obtain documentation for any price changes and request your HUD-1 settlement statement be delivered the day before your loan closes. If there are any unwarranted changes, don't proceed with the closing until they have been resolved.

- Don't be fooled by advertising schemes that sound exclusive or too good to be true. There's almost always a hitch.

In addition to the outline provided above, you should use the MYOM Shopping Checklist to guide you through the process (in chapter 8 and in the appendices at www.mindyourownmortgage.com).

Automate the shopping process

You can conduct the entire shopping process by logging onto www.mindyourownmortgage.com. Use the online system at the Web site to obtain clear, concise, and accurate price quotes and realize significant savings. The Web site enables your personal shopping experience by:

- Automating the exchange of information with each lender you shop
- Storing quotes in your personal account
- Comparing quotes to determine the best price

You can conduct the entire shopping process by logging onto www. mindyourown mortgage.com.

Mastering the shopping process is only part of the equation. You must also actively monitor your mortgage debt, refinancing only when it's economically beneficial to do so. Managing your mortgage is a process that will continue for as long as you have one, and the more you know about it, the earlier you'll become mortgage free.

Let's learn all about it.

INSIDER VIEWPOINT:
Don't Return to the Old Ways

The credit markets narrowed considerably as a result of the onslaught of the mortgage crisis, and they worsened as the resulting recession dug deeper. This cycle will eventually be relieved, and with it the secondary market for mortgages will slowly return.

When it does, so will the range of mortgage products and credit being offered. Future evolutions in the market shouldn't change your stance to stick with fixed-rate financing. As a matter of fact, if you have a mortgage with a fixed rate of 5.5 percent or less, chances are this will be the last mortgage you will ever hold (unless you move or do something silly like tap the equity in your home with a new mortgage).

The principles taught in this book are *timely* and *timeless*—timely due to the attention brought on by crisis and timeless because they apply to all market conditions and are based on fundamental financial truths.

If sticking with what's best means you have less to show for it, so be it. The economy is excessively dependent on consumer spending and returning to the old ways—borrowing and spending without saving for the future: *will not* restore our country. Don't ever forget what happened as a result of the meltdown and what led to it: excessive consumption fueled by free-flowing credit. All those who thought they had something to show for it no longer do.

It's a very tough lesson but one that was necessary for the long-term health of our economy. We need to save first, live within our means, and protect our financial futures. Giving into consumerism is just going to put households right back where they were before the meltdown: broke on paper. And broke on paper leads to broke in the household, broke in the bank, and broke as a nation.

MANAGE IT

16

Minding Your Mortgage Means Managing It

Jerry and Cathy: Being Led Instead of Leading

Jerry and Cathy have a nice home and good jobs. They have a fair amount of savings and take the time to budget their finances. However, despite the fact their mortgage is their single largest debt, they don't think about it much. As a matter of fact, the only time it comes up in a significant way is when their mortgage broker calls on them to inform them it's time to refinance.

Jerry and Cathy appreciate the service and have referred their broker to many friends. They've refinanced several times, always lowering their payment and obtaining a better interest rate. During this time, they've been sold an adjustable-rate mortgage when rates were favorably low in 2004 and were fortunate enough to have the equity and income to refinance when rates spiked upward, then taking a fixed-rate mortgage—and yet another one in 2009 when rates hit rock bottom.

With the last refinance, the broker became Jerry and Cathy's hero. Although the advice of the broker seems to have worked out, Jerry and Cathy have made some big mistakes. While they've lowered their payments, they have paid a fair amount in fees and costs each time, and they have extended their mortgage payoff date well into their retirement years. Not once during this time did Jerry and Cathy shop the deal teed up by the broker. How do they know they've obtained a great price? Did it make sense to refinance each time along the way? They paid a hefty sum to buy down the rate into the 4 percent range, and their payment is at an all-time low.

They are being led instead of leading, and it's costing them money while making their broker a tidy living.

INSIDER VIEWPOINT:
The American Dream—
From Concept to Disaster

The term was first expressed by historian James Truslow Adams in 1931 as "that dream of a land in which life should be better and richer and fuller for everyone, with opportunity for each according to ability or achievement."

The American Dream is a national ethos in which our democratic society is seen as the source of the promise of prosperity. It has become a synonym for home ownership, since homes are seen as a status symbol derived from such prosperity. While it is arguably true some have been prevented from pursuing the American

Dream due to racial or societal injustices, it does not make it so that the government should step beyond legislating equal housing *opportunity* by ensuring home ownership across America. These are two entirely different things.

One's "ability or achievement" most often leads to the realization of the American Dream. And while we should strive for a society void of inequity, it doesn't mean we must provide for equal access to housing for those who do not have the economic means to acquire it. Yet this is precisely what the government has done over the years, with the introduction of affordable housing programs, by pressuring banks and the mortgage industry to provide a wider variety of credit, and by creating insurance programs to use taxpayer money to reimburse investors for a portion of their losses in the event an affordable housing market goes south.

This, combined with the explosive growth of the subprime credit industry, contributed to the housing bubble by helping to artificially inflate housing prices and by putting people into homes that they could not afford.

The American Dream was never meant to imply everyone should own a home. As a matter of fact, it wasn't meant to imply home ownership at all. In reality, it resulted in overinflated expectations that were mistakenly taken on by government to provide to its citizenship and later used by the free market as a concept upon which to capitalize.

As declared by our founders, our Creator has bestowed upon us certain inalienable rights, including "Life, Liberty and the Pursuit of Happiness." Society's connection of happiness to material possessions and the misapplication of the thinking behind the

term "The American Dream" are at the root of what has led to
economic disaster.

Managing your mortgage means you stay focused on the end result,
becoming mortgage free. This entails the following:

- Shop in a manner that forces commodity pricing.
- Manage your monthly expenses, using your discretionary
  dollars to pay down debt.
- Never refinance unless you can lower the cost of your debt
  and pay off your debt earlier.

Over the long run, this strategy will yield huge dividends. The
key phrase in this sentence is *over the long run*. Because of the long-
term nature of your mortgage debt, the monthly spending decisions
you make and the approach you take when refinancing your mortgage debt will have an immense impact on your ability to become
mortgage free. You must retain a long-term mind-set and deploy
this into your monthly, short-term decisions.

You'll make better financial decisions as long as you keep the
endgame in mind: paying off your mortgage. Wealth isn't measured solely based on your assets; it's measured by the absence
of liabilities (monies you owe). If you don't have liabilities, you
obtain the freedom to spend your time as you choose. You can't do
that if you end up strapped to a mortgage when you're sixty-five
years old.

The American Dream is like freedom: it cannot be borrowed.
Our freedom as Americans has been purchased and paid for with

the bravery of those who fought for it—many to the death. Being leveraged isn't the American Dream. Neither is owning a home. *Having paid for your home?* Now that's the American Dream.

The problem with most home owners is they don't take into consideration wealth-building decisions when determining what to do with the money that's left over after they pay their bills. Your mortgage plays a significant role in how you spend this money because each month you have the option to reduce your mortgage debt. This will save you thousands of dollars in interest along the way and accelerate your mortgage payoff date.

Most home owners don't think about their mortgages unless they are cutting the check for the monthly payment (which isn't so much fun to think about if the payment is getting out of hand) or they are reacting to some prod from a lender telling them it's a great time to refinance (which sounds good if it's going to reduce your payment). These home owners have not created a sound refinance

> ***Being leveraged isn't the American Dream. Neither is owning a home.* Having paid for your home?** *Now that's the American Dream.*

strategy. They don't have the tools to help them determine when to refinance and what to do with the enhanced monthly cash flow (which is all too often referred to as monthly *savings*). Instead, they allow the mortgage industry to lead their decisions, acting only when a lender tells them why it's a great time to refinance. That's not in your interests—it's in the lender's interests. You can't count on anyone else to make refinance decisions for you. Proper stewardship over your home, your mortgage, and your finances is your responsibility. It therefore stands to reason you should obtain the appropriate level of knowledge to make wise decisions.

The Proper Mind-Set

Gaining the proper mind-set starts with asking two questions: *Why do I have mortgage debt? and How is mortgage debt different from any other type of debt?*

Why do I have mortgage debt?

Here are some good reasons to incur mortgage debt:

- I don't have the cash to buy a home outright.
- I can afford to buy, so I'd rather own than rent because my payments remain fixed while rents increase over time.
- Mortgage interest is tax deductible, therefore further reducing the cost of my fixed payments versus renting.
- I'm using mortgage debt to purchase a long-term asset—my home, which will appreciate in value in the long run.
- If interest rates decline, I can further reduce the cost of owning my home by refinancing into a new fixed-rate mortgage and dumping the difference in the payment right back into paying down my debt.
- Over time, my fixed payment will become a smaller and smaller part of my monthly expenses, creating more and more room to invest in my family's future and easing the pressure on my monthly finances.
- As I reduce the cost of my mortgage debt, I create additional margin between the cost of that debt and the long-term

rates of return for my investments (my 401(k), college savings plans, and so on). This further enhances the return on the first 10 percent of income I must save, since my savings are essentially financed by my mortgage debt.

How is mortgage debt different from any other type of debt?

Mortgage debt finances an asset that will appreciate in the long run at a rate that exceeds the cost of the debt. I know that seems hard to believe given the housing crisis, but it's true—assuming you don't buy too much home, stick with fixed-rate financing, and avoid getting in over your head. The housing crisis is a once-in-a-lifetime event, and it does not invalidate the benefits of owning a home.

Take a look at the rest of your debts. Do they enhance your future wealth prospects? There isn't a good reason to incur any debts other than a mortgage, a car loan (because you need a car to get to work), a student loan, or a loan to fund a dire emergency (such as a health issue). Consumer debt *always* detracts from wealth. To the extent you use it, you are upside down from day one. If you refinance your mortgage and take cash out to tap your home equity, you've created consumer debt. It's disguised as mortgage debt, but its character has not changed.

Minding Your Mortgage

Minding your mortgage debt means that you actively manage it. It means you are committed to minimizing the amount of mortgage debt you take on and consistently working to eliminate it.

There are three principles to employ that will help you accomplish this goal:

1. Own your home; don't let it own you.
2. Convert your monthly spending into wealth.
3. Deploy a sound refinance strategy.

You'll learn about each of these in the ensuing chapters.

17

Own Your Home, Don't Let It Own You

Carlo and Ingrid:
A Home Is to Be Lived In, Not Lived From

My parents came to America in 1959 after meeting in Canada. Being from Europe, they witnessed firsthand the horrors of World War II, recovered, and came to this country with a much different perspective on life and money. Having lived on the run, staying in places like an abandoned train boxcar for days on end, my mother knows a few things about living on little.

I remember two things from childhood that disturbed my parents about life in the United States: that people used credit so liberally without thinking about tomorrow, and that they ate fast food! This book is about the former and while the latter is an entirely different subject, they speak to the same issue. We'll sacrifice our finances for the convenience of having what we want today, and we'll sacrifice our health for the convenience of eating on the run. My parents didn't buy things unless they had the cash to pay for them, and we sat at the dinner table nightly to a home-cooked meal as a family (without the television blabbering in the background).

It didn't matter that we had a small house—my sister and I didn't feel cramped. My father didn't make a fortune. He worked, kept the bills down, and paid off his mortgage so he could enjoy life with my mom and his grandchildren without the burden of debt. They still live in the same small home they bought in 1968, and they never borrowed more than the original mortgage to buy the home.

My parents are much the same as those who experienced the Great Depression, or anyone who was handed down the notion of a hard day's work and the importance of saving for the future. These people don't live in anticipation of buying a bigger home or acquiring things today and paying for them tomorrow. They appreciate what they have, and they don't want to be beholden to the bank for anything.

My parents escaped a war-torn existence and appreciate all the important things life has to offer. They own a home to live in it, *not to live off it.*

Your reasons for owning a home and how you use it in relation to your finances have a great impact on how you manage your mortgage debt. If you believe, for example, that home equity should be used rather than just sitting there, you'll consume at higher levels, using your mortgage debt to finance big-ticket items. This might create a stable of possessions, but hopefully you can see that it won't create wealth and the freedom to enjoy it. Certainly, the economic meltdown has made this point painfully clear.

It is imperative that you strip away the emotional component of owning a home if you are going to be successful with your finances. The emotional component drives bad financial decisions such as the following:

- Squeezing yourself into too much home, rather than taking on what's adequate (squeezing into a smaller place is a better decision)
- Making room additions you can't afford
- Putting in a pool and going into debt to do it
- Using your equity to buy big-ticket items in order to satisfy your quest for possessions

You must remain objective with your finances. Besides the obvious good emotional reasons—a place to call your own where you can raise your family—there are two objective reasons to own a home: owning a home provides you with a hedge against inflation, and it provides you with long-term, partially tax-free asset appreciation.

Inflation

For the vast majority of us, our mortgage payment is our largest monthly cash outlay. By fixing the monthly payment, a home owner enjoys housing on an inflation-proof basis. Most everything else associated with home ownership will increase over time—utilities, insurance, and so forth—yet the monthly payment can be fixed. As time wears on, the payment becomes more and more affordable, at some point becoming much less than rent for a comparable property.

Renters don't have the protection against inflation a home owner enjoys (assuming the home owner manages his mortgage debt wisely). One of the primary financial motivations for buying a home is that it protects you from the cost of escalating rents.

In order to understand more about how you are protected against inflation, let's look at a mistake. One of the primary ways trouble begins is when a home owner uses an adjustable-rate mortgage (ARM) in order to save money when rates are low.

Interest rates are usually lower when the economy is slow or struggling. As the economy recovers and inflation becomes a risk, the Federal Reserve will increase interest rates, which will generally increase mortgage rates and the payment on an ARM. Thus, as inflation cycles upward, so does your mortgage payment. The ARM works against you during periods of inflation—this is one of the reasons to stick with fixed-rate financing.

Appreciation

Over time, your home will appreciate in value. Home equity starts with a healthy down payment and fixing your mortgage payment, and is built by way of general appreciation and the repayment of mortgage debt. This is a simple concept, but it takes a long-term perspective in order to see its value.

Even if you bought at the top of the market prior to the housing crash, in the long run, the value of your property has a good chance of recovering. This is a difficult concept to grasp, especially in markets where housing values have crashed 30 percent or more. Keep in mind the declines are driven by extreme economic circumstances that will not remain in place forever; they do not invalidate the concept of long-term appreciation.

Home appreciation will return, as will the credit markets, and along with that, the ability to borrow against your home equity. If you work hard to pay down your mortgage debt, you will become naturally resistant to these forces, since giving in will undo what you worked so hard to achieve.

When you sell your home, the federal tax law currently allows a married couple up to $500,000 to be taken tax-free ($250,000 for individuals). This enhances the appreciation component, especially in retirement. A married couple can downsize and sock away half a million dollars to help fund their retirement years.

While appreciation is nice, don't count on it as your only source of retirement—you have to live somewhere. The housing crisis has changed this, but prior to the crash, too many home owners decided to forgo saving for retirement because their home equity gave them the illusion of wealth. Stick with this simple concept: your home is not a vehicle to fund retirement. If you do this, you'll be motivated to save and any appreciation in value will be icing on the cake.

> *Stick with this simple concept: your home is not a vehicle to fund retirement.*

If you understand home ownership in the context of hedging inflation and providing appreciation, the cost will be minimized and your chances of producing wealth will be maximized. You will enjoy the benefits of a fixed monthly payment, adding to it as your income increases over time, and you'll own your home to own it. It will never own you.

INSIDER TIP:
Don't Get Caught Up over Tax Benefits

I didn't list the mortgage-interest tax deduction as a primary reason for home ownership. Tax benefits are inherent to the equation of your net monthly housing cost as a home owner, but they don't merit buying a home on their own accord. From a financial standpoint, market conditions, long-term appreciation potential, and the cost of all things associated with home ownership (including tax benefits) are to be taken together in the buy-versus-rent decision. The tax benefits associated with your mortgage are the least of these because they wane over time as you pay down your debt (since your interest charges will decline). This is a good thing, since you want to pay down your debt—all tax benefits aside!

People seem to get all caught up with the tax deductions a mortgage offers. I once had a person tell me she wanted to get a larger mortgage because she needed the tax deduction. That didn't make any sense to me! I asked her what she thought her tax rate was, and she estimated it to be 30 percent. I then posed the question, "So you want to spend one dollar to save thirty cents? Sounds to me like you'll be spending an extra seventy cents."

I think you get the point.

18

CONVERT YOUR MONTHLY SPENDING INTO WEALTH

Ken and Jeri: Get Real and Start Now

Ken and Jeri don't have a financial plan. There's nothing formal about their home budgeting process, other than keeping a general eye on the bank balance, putting away 5 percent of their earnings in Ken's 401(k), and setting aside money when they can.

Problem is, "when they can" never seems to happen. Every month they find something to spend their money on. They never think about the cost of their spending, other than the cost of acquiring what they desire. Once their money is traded for the latest gadget, some new clothes, something nice for the home, a vacation to Hawaii—you name it—it's forgotten.

Ken and Jeri's monthly spending is going to drive them to the poor house. Although they're better off than most—they don't have credit card debt and have only modest car loans—without a plan they are wasting their opportunity to build wealth with each passing month. Months quickly turn into years and by the time they realize what they've done, it's going to be too late. Ken's in his late forties and they have twenty-five years left to pay on their mortgage. That pushes Ken into his seventies by the time they finally pay off their house.

While Ken doesn't believe in retiring—he plans to pursue full-time volunteer work when he retires—he's dreaming if he thinks for a moment he's going to be able to afford to volunteer. He and Jeri need to get that mortgage out of the way and they need to start working on it now. Little do they realize the huge impact they can make by dedicating their extra cash to paying down their mortgage—if only they could see the light.

Ken and Jeri need to get real and start now!

Eliminating your debts doesn't happen overnight. You must begin by trimming your expenses and making it a priority to pay down your debt on a monthly basis. Each month you pay it down, you add another layer of interest savings and you accelerate the date you'll be debt free. Each monthly decision to chip away at it rather than to spend builds momentum, and before you know it, you'll see your debts evaporate before your eyes.

The secret to becoming mortgage free is as follows:

- Shop on price, not payment.
- Pay extra on your mortgage each month.
- Refinance only when it saves you money.

You've learned how to shop. This chapter is about the second step. Let's dig in.

The Implications
of Your Monthly Spending Decisions

Go back to the list of spending priorities under the Give, Save, and Live approach discussed in chapter 5. Under this plan, you live on 80 percent of what you earn and you prioritize what you live on as follows:

1. Your home: your mortgage, property taxes, insurance, utilities, and other necessary expenses
2. Groceries
3. Adequate clothing
4. Adequate transportation and related expenses
5. Pay down debts
6. Family and relationship-building activities
7. Education not included in college savings
8. Leisure activities and hobbies
9. "Nice to haves"—an extra cell phone, MP3 player, etc.
10. Luxury items

Items one through four are necessities. After this point, there are three choices with the money that's left each month (your discretionary income):

- Pay down debts (item 5)
- Save more money (the list assumes you have saved 10 percent of your income)
- Skip it and spend it

In order to create wealth (remember how we've defined it), you must constantly review the implications of your monthly spending decisions. This is because all discretionary spending has a cost associated with it.

Let's demonstrate this by way of example. Assume you have the following debts:

- You have $5,000 in credit card debt at an 18 percent interest rate. You will pay it off within five years.
- You have a mortgage with an original balance of $350,000 at 6.5 percent with twenty-five years left to pay.

Imagine that you've been able to squeeze $350 out of the month and you decide to spend it rather than pay down your debts. The following table shows you the cost of this decision, depending upon whether you had otherwise paid down the credit card or your mortgage:

	Credit Card	Mortgage
Amount spent	$350	$350
Interest rate	18%	6.5%
Cost of not paying down	$315	$1,402 *

* Before income tax ramifications

Because you have twenty-five years left to pay on your mortgage, the interest savings far exceeds that of the credit card debt. The point of this exercise is to alert you to the long-term cost of your mortgage debt, yet you must not infer that it is better to pay down your mortgage than your credit cards. Credit card debt has a nasty habit of sticking around because you aren't forced to pay it off. You could easily find yourself carrying credit card debt for years, even decades. It's terrible and expensive—and the smart consumer will pay it off and never carry a balance again.

Here's the point you must grasp: *your spending is financed by your debt*. In this example, it costs you 18 percent to spend your money. Put another way, you aren't paying 18 percent on what you bought with your credit card, you are paying 18 percent for the privilege of using your own money because the credit card company has a claim on it. The $350 isn't yours, it's *theirs*, and they are happy to let you keep it as long as you keep paying them 18 percent. If you think of it this way, it's readily apparent this is a rotten deal.

Now that I have your attention, let's assume you don't have any credit card debt. Now your spending is financed by your mortgage. And it's *still* very expensive.

Cancelling Interest and Gaining Time

Your mortgage costs you time and money. Time spent working to make sure you can make your payment and, obviously, money in the form of interest. If you get in over your head, you'll spend precious time dealing with your mortgage when you could be spending it with loved ones. If you don't plan ahead, you'll carry the mortgage burden well into your retirement years, a time that should be mortgage free.

When you pay down mortgage debt, you cancel all future related interest charges—and that saves you *loads* of money. In order to illustrate, assume you have twenty-eight years left to pay on a $350,000 thirty-year mortgage at 6.5 percent, and you come across an extra $3,000 after you file your income taxes. You decide to spend this money on some new furniture rather than using it to pay down your mortgage:

Description	Amount
Mortgage balance in month 24	**$ 342,272**
Remaining interest on your mortgage	$ 403,252
Less: Remaining interest after paying an extra $3,000	$ 388,182
Interest cancelled	**$ 15,070**

Had you used the $3,000 to pay down your mortgage debt, you would have cancelled $15,070 of interest over the life of your mortgage and your mortgage would be paid off almost one year early. It therefore costs you $18,070 ($3,000 plus $15,070) to buy the furniture, because you are financing this purchase by not paying down your mortgage. The true cost of the furniture is multiplied by a factor of six! Would you pay $18,000 for a couch and a love seat so you can sit and watch high-definition TV?

I don't know about you, but I can experience more fulfilling high definition by going outside and doing something active, rather than sitting on my couch (as long as I wear my glasses).

When you use your money to pay down your mortgage, you reduce the cost and the term of your mortgage. You cancel interest and gain time! You need to grasp this concept: *cancelling interest and gaining time is the path to elimination of your mortgage.*

How you use the discretionary dollars you have at the end of the month dictates your success. Whether it's a large or small amount, the savings build and the payoff date accelerates as you add to your payment each month, since they create a compounding effect. It's what I call the *mortgage snowball.*

The Mortgage Snowball

The snowball concept as it relates to paying off debt isn't anything new. However, it is dramatically amplified when applied to mortgage debt, and I'm going to demonstrate a unique way of looking at this.

Let's start by imagining you are standing on a mountaintop. You decide to build a snowball. It starts with the size of a baseball, but as you pack on more snow and then roll it along, it quickly begins to grow. Layer upon layer is added as you roll it around, creating more surface area upon which to build size.

Now imagine it's large enough to send rolling down the mountain. You push it off the edge and it gains momentum as it gains size. This momentum translates into speed, and the snowball continues to grow in size at the same time. Before you know it, it's massive and it's blazing down the mountain. It'll reach the bottom in no time. It might even turn into an avalanche.

Think of the mortgage snowball like this: the increase in size represents the accumulation of interest savings as you make additional

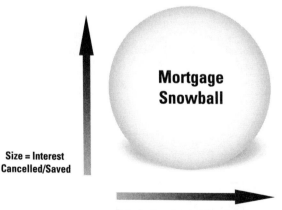

235

principal payments, and the speed represents the related acceleration of the payoff date.

I'm going to teach you how to turn your mortgage snowball into an avalanche over the next two chapters. We have to start small, so let's begin by examining how interest is calculated on a mortgage loan.

How Mortgage Interest Is Calculated

Your payment is figured at the amount that will be required to pay off your mortgage over the term provided, usually thirty years (or 360 months). Each month, your lender takes interest from your payment based upon the principal balance at the beginning of the month of your loan. The remainder goes to principal. This is known as applying interest in arrears, because the payment you make on the first of each month includes interest for the prior month.

The following table shows the application of principal and interest for the first two months and every five years thereafter on a $350,000, thirty-year fixed-rate mortgage at 6.5 percent with a regular payment of $2,212.24:

Month	Beginning Balance	Payment	Principal	Interest	Ending Balance
1	$350,000	$2,212.24	$316.40	$1,895.83	$349,684
2	$349,684	$2,212.24	$318.12	$1,894.12	$349,365
60	$328,074	$2,212.24	$435.17	$1,777.07	$327,638
120	$297,318	$2,212.24	$601.76	$1,610.47	$296,716
180	$254,789	$2,212.24	$832.13	$1,380.11	$253,957
240	$195,979	$2,212.24	$1,150.68	$1,061.55	$194,828
300	$114,656	$2,212.24	$1,591.19	$621.05	$113,065
360	$2,200	$2,212.24	$2,200.32	$11.92	$(0)

The following chart shows the percentage of the payment applied to principal at the end of each year for the same mortgage:

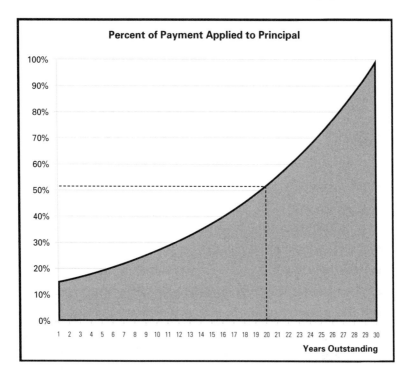

Study the schedule and the chart and you'll notice a few things:

- The amount applied to principal during the first *two-thirds* of your mortgage is far less than 50 percent of the payment amount. Check out the dotted line.
- Over time, the amount applied to principal increases dramatically, but only in the later years (and it doesn't exceed 50 percent until the last one-third of the life of the mortgage).
- The curve in the chart is relatively flat in the early years, but becomes increasingly steep. This represents the

compounding effect of principal reductions made in the early years of the mortgage.

The chart depicts the foundation for understanding the mortgage snowball. You can see the compounding effect of principal reduction by way of the increasing steepness of the curve. But this assumes you make the regular payment.

As you make additional principal payments (known as *curtailments* in the industry), you'll start with a baseball, build to boulder size, and if you stick to it, you'll cause an avalanche.

When you make a curtailment of any size, that amount will be applied to principal in the month you pay it. This immediately reduces your principal balance and reduces the amount of interest in the following and *each succeeding* month until your mortgage is paid in full. The *earlier* in the payment stream you start to make curtailments, the greater the impact will be. Making additional principal payments builds the mortgage snowball: it saves/cancels thousands in interest charges (size) and accelerates the payoff date (speed). The mortgage snowball works off the following cycle from the first month after a curtailment is applied:

The Mortgage Snowball Cycle

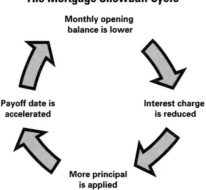

Monthly opening
balance is lower

Payoff date is
accelerated

Interest charge
is reduced

More principal
is applied

Since the process is circular, it creates a compounding effect. The mortgage snowball gains momentum. As principal is applied to your mortgage at an increasing rate, your interest savings also gather exponentially as you roll from month to month.

The One-Time Snowball

Let's look at an exaggerated example to help us witness the cycle in action. Assume you paid an extra $15,000 right out of the gate on the $350,000 fixed-rate mortgage used in our example:

1. Interest charges are reduced.

The following table compares the scheduled principal balance and cumulative interest charges (those that would occur by making the regular monthly payment) to the snowball effect (created by making the extra $15,000 payment):

Month	Scheduled		Snowball Effect		Interest Savings
	Principal Balance	Cumulative Interest	Principal Balance	Cumulative Interest	
60	$327,638	$110,373	$307,008	$104,742	$5,631
120	$296,716	$212,185	$268,188	$198,657	$13,528
180	$253,957	$302,160	$214,508	$277,711	$24,449
240	$194,828	$375,766	$140,277	$336,214	$39,551
300	$113,065	$426,736	$37,630	$366,302	$60,434
318	$82,903	$436,935	—	$368,257	$68,678
360	—	$446,406	—	$368,257	$78,149

This table shows total savings of $78,149 over the life of the mortgage for an initial investment of $15,000. That's a total return of more than five times your money—*guaranteed*. In this example, it doesn't matter if you paid an additional $15,000 or $1—the *return* is upwards of 500 percent in each case. In other words, you'll save five dollars for each dollar you pour into your mortgage. That's a nifty deal!

2. More principal is applied.

The following table compares the amount of principal applied at five-year intervals if you made the scheduled payments to the snowball effect resulting from the $15,000 curtailment:

Month	Regular Payment	Scheduled Applied to Principal	Percent	Snowball Effect Applied to Principal	Percent	Percent Improvement
60	$2,212.24	$435.17	20%	$546.32	25%	5%
120	$2,212.24	$601.76	27%	$755.46	34%	7%
180	$2,212.24	$832.13	38%	$1,044.66	47%	9%
240	$2,212.24	$1,150.68	52%	$1,444.58	65%	13%
300	$2,212.24	$1,591.19	72%	$1,997.59	90%	18%
318	$2,212.24	$1,753.68	79%	$2,201.58	100%	21%
360	$2,212.24	$2,200.32	99%			

Notice that amount applied to principal is only 5 percent better at month 60, but 9 percent better and 21 percent better by months 180 and 318, respectively. The improvement has almost doubled at these intervals, but it has *quadrupled* by the time month 318 comes around, when the mortgage is paid off early—by a full year and a half. That's the snowball effect in action!

The following chart depicts the difference between the application against principal on a yearly basis for the two scenarios over the life of each mortgage payment schedule:

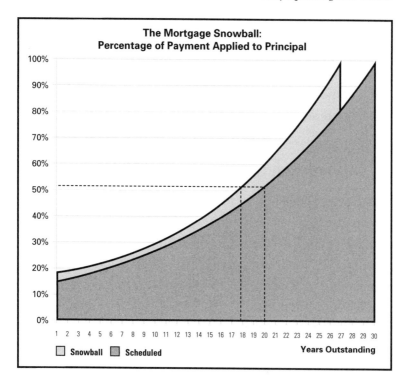

The Mortgage Snowball:
Percentage of Payment Applied to Principal

☐ Snowball ■ Scheduled   Years Outstanding

Notice the increasing steepness of the snowball curve, which results in an increasing gap between the snowball line and the scheduled line. Also, look at the dotted lines. The point at which 50 percent or more of each payment is applied to principal occurs several years earlier.

3. The payoff date is accelerated

The mortgage pays off in month 318, forty-two months earlier than scheduled.

Most of us don't have an extra $15,000 to pay on our mortgages, but we do have a few extra dollars each month and we run into larger amounts from time to time. It doesn't matter if it's $15,000 or $150, the mortgage snowball can be put into action.

Can you see how your monthly spending decisions can save or cost you thousands upon thousands of dollars? Let's study this by building a more realistic mortgage snowball.

Building a Realistic Mortgage Snowball

If you are like most people, you have a tax refund each year. And, if you are like most people, you view it as a windfall and spend it on consumer goods, a vacation, or some other item whose economic value quickly wanes. Let's suppose you are smarter than that and you plan to use your tax return to pay down your mortgage debt. Furthermore, let's presume the following:

- Your annual income tax refund averages $2,000 and the first one occurs in month seven of your new mortgage.
- You have $100 a month of discretionary cash.
- Your monthly discretionary cash increases by $25 each year.
- You decide to use your annual tax refunds and monthly discretionary cash to pay down your mortgage.

We'll use the same $350,000, thirty-year fixed-rate mortgage at 6.50 percent and see what happens in each part of the mortgage snowball cycle:

1. Interest charges are reduced.
The following table depicts collective cancelled interest as a result of the improved mortgage snowball payoff schedule:

Month	Scheduled		Accelerated		Interest Saved
	Principal Balance	Cumulative Interest	Mortgage Balance	Total Interest	
60	$327,638	$110,373	$305,521	$107,255	$3,118
120	$296,716	$212,185	$235,180	$196,149	$16,036
180	$253,957	$302,160	$128,210	$256,708	$45,452
231	**$204,964**	**$367,101**	**—**	**$275,471**	**$91,631**
240	$194,828	$375,766	—	$275,471	$100,295
300	$113,065	$426,736	—	$275,471	$151,265
360	—	$446,406	—	$275,471	$170,935

The mortgage snowball effect results in massive savings, more than $170,000!

2. More principal is applied.

This next table is a comparison of the percentages applied to principal at key intervals. The figures for the mortgage snowball payment schedule exclude the additional amount added to the payment so we can focus solely on the improvement in the amounts allocated to principal against the regular payment:

Month	Regular Payment	Scheduled		Accelerated		Percent Improvement
		Applied to Principal	Percent	Applied to Principal	Percent	
60	$2,212.24	$435.17	20%	$553.25	25%	5%
120	$2,212.24	$601.76	27%	$931.54	42%	15%
180	$2,212.24	$832.13	38%	$1,507.03	68%	30%
231	**$2,212.24**	**$1,107.98**	**50%**	**$2,212.24**	**100%**	**50%**
300	$2,212.24	$1,150.68	52%			
318	$2,212.24	$1,591.19	79%			
360	$2,212.24	$2,200.32	100%			

Take note of the stunning improvement in amounts applied to principal and the rate at which the mortgage snowball compounds. At 30 percent, the improvement in month 180 is six times better than in month 60.

The chart tells the story on a yearly basis over the life of each mortgage payment schedule: the results are nothing short of spectacular!

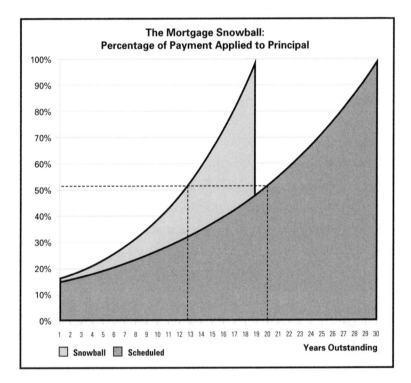

Notice the increased velocity in the steepness of the snowball curve. This demonstrates exponential application of principal over the sharply reduced life of the mortgage loan. In addition, the time it takes to reach a 50 percent principal reduction for each payment is completely inverted—it used to take *two-thirds* of the life of the mortgage to reach this threshold; now that's cut nearly in half.

3. The payoff date is accelerated.

The mortgage snowball advances the payoff date from thirty years in the future to just north of nineteen years. That's eleven years of freedom!

This example would yield even better results if the home owner did some tax planning to reduce the amount of the tax refund and spread it along the year. The $2,000 then could be applied monthly over the course of the year, chipping more off the principal, since it's put to work earlier.

This mortgage snowball is massive, but it's not an avalanche. It's missing what can be accomplished when one or more refinances are thrown into the mix. There is a specific refinance strategy that can turn your snowball into an avalanche. You'll learn all about it in the next chapter.

INSIDER TIP:
Ditch the Tax Refund

It's painful to pay taxes, but can you imagine how painful it would be if the government billed you once a year rather than withheld taxes from each paycheck? Truth is, the pain would be cast upon the government because you wouldn't have the money to pay your taxes.

For this and other reasons, the government withholds income taxes as you earn wages. The general construction of withholding and the tax collection effort result in a purposeful over withholding of *your money*. This provides the government with several advantages, including borrowing your money without paying you interest, better ensuring it collects what is legislated to be due, and creating stimulus for the economy in April and the coming months as consumers spend their tax refunds.

You have the right to reduce the amount you pay the government to ensure you pay only what is due. You have no duty to provide them with a pad nor to participate in a savings plan that doesn't pay interest. The notion that a large tax refund is a good thing is absurd. About the only value it has is to force the discipline to save (but the value of saving in this manner is highly questionable).

How's this working for our country? Don't most people just spend the money anyway?

I used $2,000 in the example above since the average federal tax refund has exceeded $2,000 for some time. I used it as an example to prove the point: you are leaving serious money on the table by allowing the government to withhold more than is due and spending your tax refund. Instead, you should reduce the amount you pay in and put that money to work as soon as it's earned.

Alternatively, you can give it to me and I'll be glad to borrow it from you interest free. I'll guarantee repayment and I'll get the money to you before April 15.

The Alternative

Saving $170,000 and shaving eleven years off one's mortgage sounds great, doesn't it? Unfortunately for most Americans, the constant messaging to consume stands in stark contrast to the silence over responsible financial habits. It's all too easy to just let it go, spend your money, and trade your future away for the temporary enjoyment of it all—play today and pay tomorrow.

In the example above, the alternative would be to have blown the annual tax refund and monthly discretionary dollars on "stuff." Nothing you can blow your money on will be worth a dime within a few years after committing the blunder. By the time twenty years have gone by, this scenario results in having nothing to show for the spending that occurred, with eleven years left to pay on a mortgage that would have otherwise been eliminated.

It's amazing that some find it's difficult to think that far ahead, yet everyone looks forward to retirement. Paying down your mortgage carries guaranteed savings results—real, spendable cash that will be available to you the day you become mortgage free. Think of the $170,000 in the example we've studied as a forced savings plan that returns monthly cash flow the day you close out your mortgage. This cash flow is the monthly mortgage payment you don't have anymore—in this case an extra $2,212 a month for just past eleven years.

A tax refund or freedom from your mortgage—what sounds better to you?

INSIDER TIP:
Generating a Retirement Cash Flow Stream

Here's a mind-bender: the example we've studied results in the mortgage being paid off 129 months early. If you take the monthly mortgage payment of $2,212, this amounts to approximately

$285,000 of spendable cash, since you won't have a mortgage payment ($2,212 times 129, rounded). How can this be, when the interest savings is only $170,000 (rounded)?

The answer lies in how you look at it. The additional payments made on the mortgage amount to $115,000. This can be viewed as a deposit against the principal portion of the payments that would remain as unpaid principal *had you not made the additional mortgage payments*. Adding the interest savings of $170,000 and the additional principle payments of $115,000 yields $285,000.

Making the additional mortgage payments in our example results in a retirement cash flow stream of $2,212 per month— for eleven years!

Don't Conform: Take a Stand Against the Culture

The culture wants to sell you the alternative—spend it all. The messaging to consume remains despite the recession we find ourselves in: our country remains too dependent on high levels of consumer spending. But now you realize what the culture wants you to buy is a rotten deal.

What you've read is not beyond the means of most households. With concerted effort, you can take your discretionary cash and achieve the kind of dramatic, wealth-creating results shown above. Start with your next tax refund: don't go and blow it on something. Use it to pay down your mortgage.

You must take a stand and exercise discipline if you wish to eliminate your mortgage debt. In this standoff there are three issues that people commonly struggle with:

1. There is no instant gratification.

Because your mortgage payment stays the same, your cash flow does not increase as you work toward becoming mortgage free. You must overcome the fact that your payment does not change. The benefits derived in the future are worth the delayed gratification.

2. You must remain committed.

Achieving results requires monthly focus on your spending—resisting the urge to forgo the benefits of paying down your mortgage debt. It's difficult to commit to an accelerated mortgage repayment plan when there are so many temptations to do otherwise.

3. A little bit doesn't seem like much.

Whether you have an extra $10 or $1,000 in any given month, take it and pay down that mortgage. No amount is too small, as the returns over time are great. Don't buy into believing it's not worth it if all you have is $75 in a particular month. Don't underestimate the power of making additional principal payments—every little bit counts.

It will take a concerted effort to stay true to the cause. The good news is that there's help in store.

Build Your Own Mortgage Snowball

The Mind Your Own Mortgage Web site provides you with tools that will facilitate your journey. You can determine what all of this means to you by logging onto www.mindyourownmortgage.com, where you can model different scenarios using your personal mortgage information. With the Mortgage Minder Dashboard, you can build your own mortgage snowball. Simply enter your mortgage information and you'll be able to monitor your debt with the end in mind.

By visiting the Web site each month and using the Mortgage Minder Dashboard, you can manage and monitor your mortgage debt:

1. Set up and track additional principal payments.
2. Determine the amount of interest saved over the life of the loan.
3. View the accelerated payoff date resulting from principal payments.
4. Perform "what if" analyses, such as:
   - Modeling the benefit of adding to your monthly principal payment on a one-time or ongoing basis
   - Calculating the cost of spending should you decide to forgo paying down your mortgage
5. Keep track of your progress:
   - Keep track of the compounding increase in amounts applied to principal
   - View your cumulative interest savings
   - Monitor the day you'll become mortgage free

The Mortgage Minder will give you the kind of instant gratification that's good for you: knowing how much you'll save by pouring extra cash into your mortgage and keeping track of the accelerated payoff date. You'll witness the results in real time as they pile up, and you'll watch your mortgage snowball grow bigger and bigger as it crashes through the barriers to financial freedom.

INSIDER VIEWPOINT:
There Are Only Three Choices

You only have three choices with your discretionary cash:

1. Spend it
2. Use it to pay down debt
3. Invest it

You may be thinking, "Isn't investing your money a better choice than paying down mortgage debt?"

Think about your mortgage like a bank thinks about deposits: the bank pays interest to its depositors and lends money to borrowers at a higher rate. The difference between the cost of deposits and the rate earned is referred to as the bank's *interest rate spread.* If you invest, it stands to reason you must earn a positive spread. In our example, this means the return on your investments must exceed 6.5 percent (the rate on the mortgage).

Keep in mind the example we used assumes you are living on 80 percent of what you make and assumes household spending is properly prioritized. If you like certainty, paying down mortgage debt is never a bad choice. The return on the dollars invested is guaranteed. That sounds pretty good these days!

When you use discretionary cash for anything other than paying down your mortgage debt, you must keep in mind this financial decision is financed by your mortgage debt. It should be clear to you by now that spending is the worst of all alternatives, which leaves you with investing or paying down your mortgage.

19

DEPLOY A SOUND REFINANCE STRATEGY

Jim and Debbie:
One Blown Refinance After Another

Jim and Debbie have what they believe to be a solid financial plan. They sock away 15 percent of their earnings in their 401(k), give a fair bit to charity, and are on track to send both of their children to college.

They have a solid understanding of what to do with everything but their mortgage debt. Like many, who seem to have a comprehensive financial plan, their plan doesn't include specific guidance concerning the proper circumstances under which they should refinance their mortgage. They've refinanced several times over the past eight years for a variety of reasons, including tapping their home equity to make a room addition, paying off their car loans, and lowering their interest rate when the market allowed them to do so. All of the refinances, except for the time they took out cash to complete the room addition, were at the solicitation of their mortgage broker.

There's no strategy involved here, other than responding to their broker. They've lowered their payments over time, which freed up extra cash. Their most recent refinance will be their last—they were able to reduce their rate to 4.5 percent and see a dramatic reduction in their monthly payments. It didn't cost them a dime out of their pocket, since all the costs were rolled into the new loan.

This made it appear as if things were just dandy with the debt, but if you were to peel back the covers, you'd find they've blown one refinance after another.

If you wish to successfully manage your mortgage, you must remove the mortgage payment from any decision to refinance.

Call it deception, lack of education, or a combination of both, the same old story is sold to and bought by mortgage consumers time after time: "refinance now and save hundreds per month." If you wish to successfully manage your mortgage, you must remove the mortgage payment from any decision to refinance. This isn't optional. *Refinancing is not about lowering your payment.*

Before the Crash

Roll back the clock to 2004. Mortgage interest rates are the lowest they've been in forty years and housing prices are soaring. You owe

$300,000 on a mortgage you took out in 2001, with a fixed rate of 6.5 percent; your payment is $1,965.

Fixed rates are down to the high fives, so you decide it's time to refinance. Since your home is now worth $450,000, you decide to tap $50,000 of your home equity. Now you're looking at a $358,000 mortgage after adding closing costs. The payment on the thirty-year fixed-rate loan at 5.75 percent is $2,090, just $125 more per month.

But . . . there's a "better" deal. Your mortgage loan officer has a loan that's fixed for three years (at 4.0 percent) and the closing costs aren't any higher. The payment is only $1,709—more than $250 less than your current mortgage payment and $381 better than the thirty-year fixed-rate option. It's a no-brainer, right?

Wrong.

You've just blown your refinance; it just hasn't gone off yet. Since you know the future, you know what happens when this ticking time bomb goes off: rates skyrocket in 2007, the mortgage adjusts, the market crashes and, well . . . it's not a pretty picture. Collateral damage is everywhere.

This mortgage decision was made based upon the payment. Have we learned anything? Let's look at a typical refinance after the crash.

The 4.5 Percent Sucker Loan

As I write this, the recession of 2008 is in full force. Everyone is talking about low mortgage rates: the government, the press, advertisements, your friends, and your neighbors. Indeed, rates have dipped to the lowest they've been in some fifty years. The government is trying to revive the economy through a variety of stimulus measures, including printing money to support artificially low rates and other measures to prop up the mortgage market.

You are one of the lucky ones—you have a job and you have equity in your home. You've had your current mortgage for five years. You originally borrowed $400,000 on a thirty-year term at 5.75 percent fixed, your payment is $2,334 and you have $372,000 left to pay.

You respond to a great radio ad promising you'll save hundreds of dollars per month by refinancing at today's super-low 4.5 percent thirty-year fixed rate. You are talking to the mortgage lender on the phone and he's got a great deal for you:

- Your new payment at 4.5 percent is going to be $1,940.
- He's going to lower your rate by 1.25 percent.
- There's $11,000 in closing costs, but you can roll these costs into the new loan, resulting in a new mortgage of $383,000.

You've lowered your rate from 5.75 percent to 4.5 percent and your payment decreased by almost $394. Doesn't this sound like a great deal? Most would say yes and take it. And they would be dead wrong. Why is this?

Take a look at the following table:

	Old Loan	New Loan
Years to pay	25	30
Monthly payment	$ 2,334	$ 1,940
Total of all payments	$700,200	$698,400
Difference	**$1,800**	

When you add up all the payments, you've only saved $1,800. But the promise was that you'd save almost $400 per month. What happened?

Let's take a closer look at the underlying problem.

Description	Amount
The amount of interest you will pay if you keep your existing loan over the remaining twenty-five years	$ 328,200
The amount of interest you will pay if you refinance, signing up for another thirty years of payments	$ 315,400
Interest saved with the new loan	$ 12,800
Subtract the closing costs paid to obtain the new loan	$ 11,000
Net savings as a result of this refinance	$ 1,800

Now you see the lie baked into the pitch. What caused you to fall for it? *The lower payment*: it only creates the *illusion* that you'll save lots of money.

You paid $11,000 to reduce your rate to 4.5 percent and have accomplished nothing. But your mortgage lender sure is happy you fell for the trickery: you've lined his pockets.

Recall your spending is financed by your mortgage debt. In this case, you extended your mortgage for another five years to create the ability to spend an additional $394 per month. Because no savings have been generated, all you have done is finance the reduction in your mortgage payment against an additional five years of payments. You are essentially borrowing the money from yourself and your future.

Here's a newsflash concerning the current recession: the government and everyone that's looking to sell you something is counting on you to do this. Lower interest rates spur refinance activity and the resulting reduction in payments pumps money into the economy. Take note: the temptation of lower payments luring you to refinance

Take note: the temptation of lower payments luring you to refinance and spend is baked into the system.

257

and spend is baked into the system. It's purposeful, it's aimed at you, and it steals from your future to benefit the mortgage company and anyone you buy things from today.

The 4.5 percent sucker loan will cause pain. You might play today, but you're going to pay for it tomorrow.

If you think about it, what's different between this refinance and the behavior demonstrated by consumers prior to the meltdown? Not much, sorry to say. Prior to the crash, people used their homes as a means to consume. The 4.5 percent sucker loan accomplishes the same objective.

If you fall for this deal (or any other time you can lower your payment), you are a sucker. Everyone wins but you.

Correcting the Problem

The "bad refinance" problem exists in all interest rates cycles and mortgage markets. How do you avoid this problem? How do you know if your refinance will accomplish anything of value? Answer: Deploy the MYOM Refinance Strategy.

Only a sound refinance strategy can protect you from financial harm. Here it is—refinance only when you can accomplish the following three objectives:

1. Lower the cost of your mortgage.
2. Accelerate the payoff date.
3. Ensure you surpass break-even on total fees and the cost of anything else added to the new loan balance.

Consider the 4.5 percent sucker loan. Is it possible to take this loan and make it sucker free? What happens if you make the *old payment* of $2,334 on the new loan? Take a look at the following chart, which depicts the difference in total interest charges over the life of the loan when you make the old payment versus the new payment.

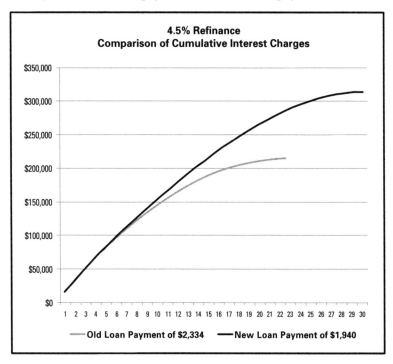

If you make the old payment on the new loan, you will accomplish two of the three objectives (assuming you stay in your home until the mortgage is paid off):

1. *You've lowered the cost of your mortgage.*

   Making the old payment of $2,334 saves you $103,000 in interest charges.
2. *You will accelerate the payoff date.*

   Your new loan pays off three and a half years earlier than the twenty-five years left to pay on the old mortgage.

Let's dive deeper to explain the concept at work. Assume the following breakdown of total fees to obtain the 4.5 percent rate:

Description	Amount
Existing mortgage balance	$372,000
Plus points and fees: Points (2.125%)	$ 7,905
Lender fees	$ 1,600
Third-party fees	$ 1,495
Total fees	$ 11,000
New loan amount	**$ 383,000**

You paid an additional $11,000 to lower your rate to 4.5 percent, which was rolled into your new loan balance. Let's consider this paid even though it's borrowed, since you now owe the money and you'll have to pay it off.

Read the following carefully, as we are at a critical juncture in our learning: When you make the old payment on the new loan, it's just as if the existing lender has lowered your rate from 5.75 percent to 4.5 percent and charged you $11,000 by adding it to your loan balance.

Do you see there would be no difference if the old lender were to make this change versus using the refinance to accomplish it? It is extremely important you grasp this concept because it underscores the problem with this and most other refinances: *you aren't forced to make the old payment once you obtain your new loan.*

If your old lender offered you the deal, you'd be forced to make your existing payment and you would surely satisfy the first two objectives. And you must satisfy the first two objectives before you can consider the refinance.

Since we pass these tests, what about the third objective? Think of it as if you had to pay the $11,000 out of your pocket. Would you do it?

Based on mathematical modeling, it would take you more than three years to recoup your $11,000 investment, after which you would begin to save money. Is three to four years an acceptable period of time over which to recoup the cost to obtain the 4.5 percent rate?

Two Years to Break Even, No More

The third objective is so important, it deserves to have a guideline applied to it. Here it is: Don't refinance unless you can recoup total fees and any other closing costs added to your loan balance inside of two years.

In our example, the existing loan at 5.75 percent is fantastic relative to historical 8 percent averages, and you would be well advised to leave it alone if it takes too long to recoup the closing costs.

Don't refinance unless you can recoup total fees and any other closing costs added to your loan balance inside of two years.

If refinancing is worth it in the first place, there will be enough of a difference between your current rate and the refinanced rate without paying a lot in closing costs. Think back to the MYOM Rate Sheet Quote. Recall that the advertised rate is most likely the lowest rate on the sheet and therefore is associated with the highest points. Perhaps there's a rate with very little cost that is lower than your current rate.

INSIDER TIP:
Don't Buy the Break-Even Sales Pitch

It's common practice for a mortgage lender to help you calculate the break-even point when addressing closing costs. Conventional thinking is to take the closing costs and divide them by the reduction in your mortgage payment. Your mortgage lender is going to point this out to justify the cost to obtain your refinance. While this is only an approximation, it doesn't really matter—it's still bad advice.

Do you notice the common theme of bad advice and bad decisions? They *always* refer to the mortgage payment. Justification of closing costs as described above is based on the reduction in the payment and distracts from the other things you must consider. As a matter of fact, you'll never break even on closing costs if the new loan costs you more in the long run than the old one!

You simply must consider the entire economic picture when refinancing.

Rounding out the MYOM Refinance Strategy

We have learned a refinance is a wise financial decision when you can accomplish *all three* of the following objectives:

1. Lower the cost of your mortgage.
2. Accelerate the payoff date.
3. Ensure you surpass break-even on total fees and anything else added to the new loan balance.

In order to ensure you remain focused on these objectives, think of a refinance in the following manner:

- Treat a refinance as if your current lender were to change your rate and require you to continue to make the same payment.
- Treat the total fees as the cost to obtain the new interest rate, not to obtain a lower payment.

In other words, a properly executed refinance is merely a charge to secure a better fixed rate that helps you pay off early. *A refinance is a tool to assist you in becoming mortgage free. Don't use it for any other purpose.* The secret to using a refinance to assist you in becoming mortgage free has now been revealed: Lower your rate for an acceptable charge and keep making your old payment.

> *A refinance is a tool to assist you in becoming mortgage free. Don't use it for any other purpose.*

Do you want to ensure you don't make mistakes on your way to eliminating your mortgage debt? Ensure you adhere to the following in addition to the three objectives:

- *Use the MYOM Shopping System.*
  Avoid getting ripped off and find the best deal.

- *Keep it simple.*
  Use only fixed-rate loans. You can't count on the savings offered by an adjustable-rate mortgage since it's impossible to predict interest rates. For this reason, you can't rely on achieving the first two objectives.

• *Never take cash out.*

If you want to pay off your debt, why take cash out with a refinance? Whatever you buy with the cash will cost you dearly in interest charges over the long run. If you don't have the money, don't buy it!

Now you have the complete MYOM Refinance Strategy: refinance based on the three objectives, use the MYOM Shopping System, keep it simple, and never take cash out.

You can apply these principles using the mortgage refinance tools at www.mindyourownmortgage.com. The tools will allow you to enter multiple scenarios and provide the necessary calculations to ensure you make wise decisions.

The Benefits of Deploying the MYOM Refinance Strategy Over Time

Very few people have the discipline to resist spending the reduction in the monthly payment a new mortgage offers. If you don't resist, you severely hamper elimination of your mortgage debt. However, if you have the fortitude to apply the MYOM Refinance Strategy, you will reap big rewards.

Let's look at an example by assuming you enter a period of declining rates. You hold a $350,000 thirty-year fixed-rate mortgage at 6.75 percent. Your monthly payment is $2,270 and you've made this payment for five years. The balance on your mortgage is now $328,565 and rates have dipped below 6 percent. You shop using the MYOM Shopping System and you obtain the following quote, which happens to be the best of three lenders (see table on page 265.)

Mind Your Own Mortgage
Rate Sheet Quote
www.mindyourownmortgage.com

Quote Date		Loan Type	Conventional
Loan Amount	$328,565	Loan Term	30 years
Lender		Amortization	Fixed
Contact Name		Escrow/Impounds	None
Contact Tel		Lock Term	30 days
Contact E-mail		Cash out?	No

Interest Rate	Points	Points ($$)	Lender Fees	Third Party Fees	Total Points and Fees	Payment
5.125%	2.250%	$ 6,750	$ 1,950	$ 1,465	$ 10,165	$ 1,788.99
5.250%	1.250%	$ 3,750	$ 1,950	$ 1,465	$ 7,165	$ 1,814.35
5.375%	0.750%	$ 2,250	$ 1,950	$ 1,465	$ 5,665	$ 1,839.87
5.500%	0.375%	$ 1,125	$ 1,950	$ 1,465	$ 4,647	$ 1,865.56
5.625%	0.000%	$ —	$ 1,950	$ 1,465	$ 3,415	$ 1,891.41
5.750%	-0.375%	$ (1,125)	$ 1,950	$ 1,465	$ 2,290	$ 1,917.42
5.875%	-1.000%	$ (3,000)	$ 1,950	$ 1,465	$ 415	$ 1,943.59
6.000%	-1.138%	$ (3,415)	$ 1,950	$ 1,465	$ —	$ 1,969.91

You have a simple decision on your hands, since you can reduce your rate from 6.75 percent to 6 percent with a full rebate (at no cost). Since you'll pay for prepaids/recurring closing costs out of pocket, your loan balance won't increase.

Consider the MYOM Refinance Strategy:

- Satisfy all three of the following objectives:
  1. Lower the cost of your mortgage
  2. Accelerate the payoff date
  3. Ensure you surpass break-even on closing costs
- Use the MYOM Shopping System to nab the best deal.
- Keep it simple: fixed-rate financing
- Never take cash out

You have achieved all of these objectives with the 6 percent full rebate loan as long as you continue to make your existing payment. Here's the result:

	Keep Old Loan	New Loan—New Payment	New Loan—Old Payment
Remaining Number of Payments	300	360	258
Payment	$2,270	$1,970	$2,270
Total of Remaining Payments	$681,000	$709,200	$585,660
Total Interest Charges	$352,435	$380,635	$257,095

The new payment is $300 less than the old payment, but it will take you an additional five years to become mortgage free and this will cost you more than $28,000 in additional interest charges.

If you make your old payment of $2,270, you accelerate the payoff date of your existing mortgage by 3.5 years (300 months minus 258 months) and you save $95,340 ($352,435 minus $257,095)!

Notice the damage that results if you succumb to making the new payment; you'll make payments for 8.5 more years (360 months instead of 258) and it will cost you $123,540 ($380,635 minus $257,095).

Let's assume rates continue to decline and you take advantage of the situation by adhering to the MYOM Refinance Strategy, refinancing three times:

1. From 6.75 percent to 6 percent at five years at no cost, as above
2. From 6 percent to 5.5 percent at seven years at no cost
3. From 5.5 percent to 5.125 percent at ten years at no cost

The following graph compares the total interest charges and payoff date if you stick with the MYOM Refinance Strategy and continue to make the $2,270 payment, versus the total interest charges and payoff date if you make the new payment each time you refinance (from the point of the first refinance at year 5):

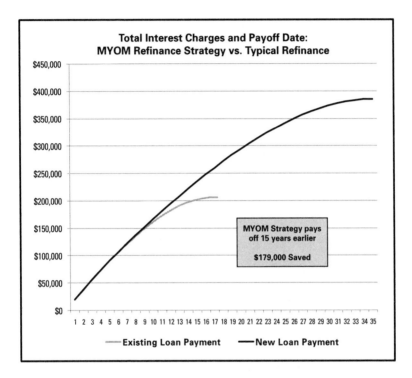

Sticking with the MYOM Refinance Strategy yields spectacular results! Now let's take a look at the payments associated with each refinance:

	Old Rate	New Rate	Original Payment	New Payments	Payment "Savings"
Refinance #1	6.750%	6.000%	$ 2,270	$ 1,970	$ 300
Refinance #2	6.000%	5.000%	$ 2,270	$ 1,814	$ 456
Refinance #3	5.500%	5.125%	$ 2,270	$ 1,670	$ 600

As the chart shows, there are no savings to be had if you make the new payments. Yet the payment savings from one refinance to the next are what the mortgage companies are going to sell. If you aren't informed, you will make a big mistake—just imagine the allure of the reduction in the payment to the uninformed.

The disastrous results of refinancing based on your payment cannot be overstated.

Turning the Mortgage Snowball into an Avalanche

If you follow the MYOM Refinance Strategy, you'll consistently reduce the cost of your debt and accelerate the payoff date. You're playing it as if you don't have a choice but to make your old payment; making the old payment adds pure principal reduction each month. But when you combine the interest-rate reduction of a properly executed refinance with an *additional* layer of principal reductions in addition to maintaining your original payment, you turn the snowball into an avalanche:

- Making additional principal payments from the onset gets the mortgage snowball rolling.
- Refinancing increases momentum by reducing the interest rate.
- The layer of additional principal reductions on top of your original payment and the interest-rate reduction work together, adding yet more momentum.
- Refinance again and the pull of gravity becomes greater.
- Now there's an additional layer of principal reductions on top of the previous layers and yet another interest

rate reduction, causing the snowball to reach massive proportions.

Refinance again and you have an avalanche on your hands. You are blazing down the mountain, unstoppable on your way to an early payoff date.

Let's apply the avalanche scenario to the previous example. We started with a $350,000 thirty-year fixed-rate mortgage at 6.75 percent and a monthly payment of $2,270 that we applied to a series of refinances over time in the example above. This saved $179,000 in interest charges and accelerated the original payoff date by fifteen years.

Assume you committed to a monthly payment of $2,500 at the onset (rather than your original payment of $2,270) until you paid off the mortgage. What happens? Conceptually, the mortgage snowball looks like this:

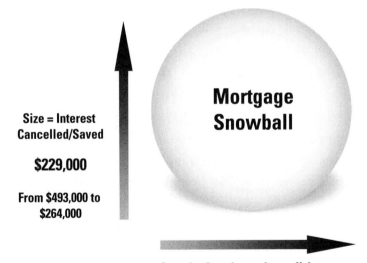

Size = Interest Cancelled/Saved

$229,000

From $493,000 to $264,000

Mortgage Snowball

Speed = Accelerated payoff date
From 40 years down to 20

By adding only another $230 to your original payment and sticking with it you have created an avalanche of savings amounting to $229,000 and cut the time to mortgage payment freedom in half! Had you made your original mortgage payment and the new payment associated with each refinance, it would have cost you almost $500,000 in interest charges after forty years of mortgage payments. If you were thirty-five years old when you started this, you will make mortgage payments until you are seventy-five years old.

Deploying the MYOM Refinance Strategy, on the other hand, has you mortgage free by fifty-five. Stunning, isn't it?

The Zero-Risk Refinance Strategy

If your lender called you and offered to lower your interest rate at no charge, would you do it? Of course you would!

Let's go back to the 4.5 percent sucker loan. In this example, you hold a $400,000 loan at 5.75 percent fixed, your payment is $2,334, and you have $372,000 left to pay. Take a look at the completed MYOM Rate Sheet Quote on page 271.

As we now know, taking the 4.5 percent rate-option loan makes you a sucker. But what about the 5.375 percent rate option?

In this case, if you refinance and make the old payment on the new loan, it's just as if your existing lender has lowered your rate from 5.75 percent to 5.375 percent and has charged you nothing to do it.

The zero-risk refinance strategy is to refinance whenever you can reduce your interest rate by at least .25 percent at no cost. If you continue to make your existing payment, you satisfy the first two refinance objectives and you don't have to think about the third objective, since there are no closing costs.

Mind Your Own Mortgage
Rate Sheet Quote
www.mindyourownmortgage.com

Quote Date		Loan Type	Conventional
Loan Amount	$372,000	Loan Term	30 years
Lender		Amortization	Fixed
Contact Name		Escrow/Impounds	None
Contact Tel		Lock Term	30 days
Contact E-mail		Cash out?	No

Interest Rate	Points	Points ($$)	Lender Fees	Third Party Fees	Total Points and Fees	Payment
4.500%	2.125%	$ 7,905	$ 1,600	$ 1,495	$ 11,000	$ 1,884.87
4.625%	1.250%	$ 4,650	$ 1,600	$ 1,495	$ 7,745	$ 1,912.60
4.750%	0.750%	$ 2,790	$ 1,600	$ 1,495	$ 5,885	$ 1,940.53
4.875%	0.375%	$ 1,395	$ 1,600	$ 1,495	$ 4,490	$ 1,968.65
5.000%	0.000%	$ —	$ 1,600	$ 1,495	$ 3,095	$ 1,996.98
5.125%	-0.375%	$ (1,395)	$ 1,600	$ 1,495	$ 1,700	$ 2,025.49
5.250%	-0.625%	$ (2,325)	$ 1,600	$ 1,495	$ 770	$ 2,054.20
5.375%	-0.832%	$ (3,095)	$ 1,600	$ 1,495	$ (0)	$ 2,083.09

INSIDER TIP:
The Debt Consolidation Sales Trap

If you have an auto loan, credit card balances, or other consumer loans, consolidating them into your mortgage generally won't save you any money. Why?

Mortgage providers commonly refer to the reduction in monthly payments as the primary benefit of consolidating other debts with your mortgage. As you know by now, making a decision based on payment will get you into trouble. Lower payments are not a benefit!

Assume you have a $5,000 credit card balance carrying interest at 18 percent. If you refinanced your mortgage and paid off the credit card debt, you'd be making payments on the $5,000 balance for thirty years. This is because each additional dollar you borrow on a mortgage is the last dollar you pay off. As a result, you'll pay interest on your old credit card balance at your mortgage rate until you make the last few payments. This costs you dearly.

If you consolidate debts, you must follow the MYOM Refinance Strategy for the new mortgage and *each loan rolled into the new mortgage*. This means you don't do it unless you reduce the cost and accelerate the payoff date of each debt.

Here's how you solve the problem:

- If you consolidate credit card debt into your mortgage, make additional principal payments each month. Set a goal to pay off the credit card debt just as if it were left unpaid (you may have paid the credit card company, but you rolled it into your mortgage: it *is* still unpaid).
- If you have an auto or other loan that carries monthly payments and you consolidate the loan, continue to make the existing payment by adding it to the monthly mortgage payment.

In other words, treat your new mortgage as if it were three loans with three separate payments you add together each month:

1. One on your house
2. One on your credit card
3. One on your car or other loan

Since your new mortgage will have a rate lower than the credit card and other loans (it better!), applying an aggressive payment schedule will pay these balances off earlier.

Never refinance other debts into your mortgage solely for the sake of reducing your payments.

Don't Make the Same Mistakes

Please don't make the same mistakes with your mortgage that are made by the uninformed. By now, I trust you are convinced these mistakes will cost you a fortune.

With the proper understanding of home ownership, demonstrating wise stewardship of your monthly discretionary cash by making contributions to an early mortgage payoff date, and deploying the MYOM Refinance Strategy to multiply the impact, you'll be mortgage free before you know it.

Log On to the Web Site

By logging on to www.mindyourownmortgage.com, you can manage your mortgage debt and deploy the MYOM Refinance Strategy. The Web site contains a refinance decision engine that performs the three tests for you:

1. Reduce the cost of your debt.
2. Accelerate the maturity date.
3. Recoup closing costs inside of two years.

Simply enter your current mortgage information and any proposed mortgage loan and the work will be done for you.

You can create your own mortgage avalanche by using the Mortgage Minder Dashboard and the refinance decision tools in concert with each other. This will allow you to monitor your mortgage debt on a monthly basis and filter whether it's appropriate to refinance your mortgage debt after you have determined the best price by using the MYOM Shopping System. You will be able to apply the principles of this book to your personal situation.

The comprehensive tools provided on the Web site will help you make independent, objective decisions that enable a path to mortgage elimination—unhindered by the mortgage industry's attack on your finances.

FINISH IT

20

MORTGAGE FREEDOM

Pete and Deborah:
At the Bottom of the Hill Before Pete's Over the Hill

Pete and Deborah have been married for ten years now. When they
first started out, they bought just enough of a home to deal with their
plans for a family without going overboard. They used fixed-rate
financing to purchase their home and after shopping the mortgage
with several lenders, found the best price (which wasn't with the broker the real estate agent had suggested), and saved more than $2,000.
A few years into the deal, they found it easier to make the payments as
Pete had advanced in his career and his income came alongside.

Since then, Pete has kept an eye on mortgage rates and, after
consulting with Deborah, has refinanced the home three times. Pete
was able to drop their interest rate each time, paying very little, if
anything, in closing costs to get it done. Each time they refinanced,
Pete and Deborah renewed their covenant to keep on making their
original payment, thereby ensuring they'd accelerate the payoff date
and save money in doing so.

Not once has Pete responded to a mailer, a radio ad, or a call from a friend's mortgage broker. Pete makes the decision to engage—and only when the time is right. He makes it a rule to shop at least three lenders, summarizes his findings by comparing the rate and total cost for each quote, and proceeds solely on the best price. Pete understands a fixed-rate mortgage is a fixed-rate mortgage and his business is going to the lowest bidder. To Pete, it's all about price, not payment.

Pete and Deborah have been able to bottom at 5.375 percent and don't see the need to refinance again. They enjoy the thought of being completely debt free. To that end, they have no credit card debt and an auto loan on Deborah's minivan (don't laugh—minivans are cool these days). Each month, after giving 10 percent, saving 15 percent, and paying their bills (they don't have many), they take another step toward mortgage freedom by stashing cash into paying down the debt. The mortgage snowball is building quickly and Pete plans to ride the avalanche to the bottom of the hill.

Pete thinks it is cool that he'll get to the bottom of the hill before he's over the hill. He and Deborah will be mortgage free by the time he's forty-five years old.

"It's Time to Think Differently"

I made the statement above at the beginning of this book. Do you recall? I wanted to write this instead:

"You Must Change the Way You Think"

But you don't wake someone up from a deep sleep by shining a spotlight in his face—you slowly turn up the lights.

The mortgage industry has consumers right where they want them: deeply asleep at the switch. This puts the industry in control of when to flip on the lights and sell you a refinance. The bright lights don't offend you because no one is challenging your thought process. Rather, the industry appeals to your senses and everything you've been led to believe about mortgages. Grab the lower payment—it's a good thing!

But now you know better. You know the single most common mistake made by consumers is to decide on payment. You understand this leads to all sorts of trouble: you'll be exposed to hidden charges, additional fees, slick and undetected sales tactics, price changes you can't reconcile, additional interest charges costing you thousands over the life of the loan, mortgage payments well into your retirement years, and bondage to your mortgage debt.

You understand now that you won't save money just because you lowered your mortgage payment.

You understand that you'll make a bad decision.

The cultural pull to refinance and spend is strong, but now that you understand the damage it causes and the benefits of avoiding it, you should be able to resist. All you need to do is adopt the teachings of this book and maintain a disciplined approach that is rooted in sound financial stewardship.

Now it's time to finish it. It's time to apply what you have learned and enable your personal path to becoming mortgage free.

Get a Grip on It

If you own a home, you must usually carry a mortgage. That mortgage will play an integral role in your overall financial picture, making it look bright or bleak depending upon how you manage this debt.

The credit crisis that began in 2007 had its roots in the decisions we made as consumers long before the storm hit our shores. The poor decisions of some in the industry, government, and our society gave rise to consequences for the rest of us, but we played our part. In practical terms, there isn't any such thing as a bailout, because someone's got to pay.

Capitalism and the free markets created it and they can fix it. Our society needs to make adjustments and each of us needs to do our part: we must live within our means.

A home is meant to be lived in as an affordable necessity. It isn't meant to provide an avenue to acquire debt to finance purchases that your income doesn't support.

Owning a home is a long-term prospect that requires you to manage the various aspects of the investment (your home) and the related mortgage debt. Your goal should be to build equity over time and fix the cost of housing as a hedge against inflation. The only means to accomplish this is to employ fixed-rate financing. No other mortgage debt instrument will give you the security and certainty that a fixed-rate mortgage provides.

The dangers of adjustable-rate mortgages are evident to all with hindsight, but are based upon very clear and predictable economic principles. Interest rates will increase during times of inflation, which gives rise to flattening or declining housing prices. These circumstances can block the highly leveraged borrower from refinancing out of rising mortgage loan payments, threatening his ability to stay in the home. Recent history proves this risk at a magnitude so great the damage was complete and final by the time interest rates were adjusted in an effort to cure the problem.

This recession reminds us that we must get right with our finances.

Returning to the old ways isn't going to cut it: our economy was broke before it went bust. A nation comprised of unsustainable household economies is destined to fail. You must begin by taking a stand against the culture of consumption and prioritize your spending so as to leave room for what's most important in life—people. Adopting the Give, Save, and Live spending plan will set your financial ship straight and allow you to weather the storms that are an inevitable component of life. It will help you rearrange your spending habits in a fashion that sets you apart from the culture of consumerism.

Debt plays a role in your finances in a supportive or destructive manner. It's supportive when it's associated with adequate housing and transportation, destructive when it's associated with consumption. Consumer debt opens the door to spending beyond your means. It costs you far more in the long run than the enjoyment you'll obtain from the purchases you made. If you have more consumer debt than cash reserves, you effectively have no cash. This is because the cost of the debt exceeds the rate at which your cash can be invested safely. Until you understand this, you'll continue to erode your finances without saving anything for the future.

Any form of debt represents a current and future claim on your money. As a matter of fact, it's their money even though it's sitting in your bank account—which is why they make you pay dearly for the privilege of using it. If you don't have the cash to pay for it, don't buy it. Pay off those consumer debts instead and put yourself in position to tackle your mortgage before it tackles you. The mortgage industry is designed to keep you in perpetual debt, enslaved to their prompts to refinance when it's in their best interests to reach out to you.

Mortgages are made of money and money is a commodity.

Unfortunately, mortgages are priced as a commodity throughout the food chain, with the exception of the interface with you.

Getting a grip means you need to become educated so you can make informed decisions—it starts by understanding how to avoid troubled mortgage debt:

- Never buy on payment.
- Don't ask how much you qualify for, determine how much you can afford.
- Build your cash reserves to at least six months of expenses.
- Don't buy the ability to consume by refinancing to lower your payment.
- Don't get sucked into the allure of introductory interest rates.
- Ignore the attempts to convince you when it's right to refinance.
- Never tap home equity.
- Beware of the commissioned salesperson.

Stick to your guns. Make it your objective to pay off your mortgage and do all you can to avoid a mortgage crisis along the way.

Shop for It

Transparency, simplicity, and certainty. Wouldn't it be great if you could shop for a mortgage under these circumstances?

You can. The information is available and the MYOM Shopping System provides you with the tools to make it happen. But first you need to set the ground rules and you must prepare yourself:

- Keep it simple—the terms of a fixed-rate mortgage can be described in one sentence. That's simplicity. Certainty comes from the fixed nature of the payments. Take out a fixed-rate mortgage and you have something you can count on that will become more affordable over time.

- Prepare for a fight—shopping for a mortgage as an informed consumer is like stepping into the ring. Most are going to fight to sell you in the traditional fashion. You must turn the tables and engage in an objective pursuit to obtain the information you need to make an independent decision. Review the top ten shopping tactics listed at the end of chapter 8 before you go about obtaining a quote.

The MYOM Shopping System forces commodity-type pricing so you can easily compare quotes. Once you've obtained the right information it's like shopping for a gallon of gas.

An automated version of the system is available at www.mind yourownmortgage.com. Use it to enable the shopping process:

- Use the MYOM Rate Sheet Quote to obtain a complete quote from at least three lenders on the same day. All the quotes need to be for the same type of loan and terms.

- E-mail your MYOM Shopping System forms to your lender and gain his commitment to complete the quote online in the format provided.

- If you meet resistance while shopping, don't back down. If a lender doesn't cooperate or insists upon selling you without disclosing the full range of price using the MYOM forms, *walk away.*

- Ensure you use the same loan and rate-lock assumptions for each quote you obtain. Lock your rate as soon as possible. There's no sense in playing the market, since you have no idea where it's heading. Besides, floating your rate exposes you to price manipulation.
- Complete a full mortgage application with each lender. Remember, you don't have to pay a dime to obtain the quote. If the lender wants to charge you anything, forget it and move on.
- Request the following documentation to be returned for your quote, along with what is required by law:
  - MYOM Shopping System forms
  - The Good Faith Estimate (GFE) for a chosen rate
  - Written rate-lock policy
- Review the quotes for reasonableness, ensuring you've obtained a MYOM Quote Detail form from each lender. For each rate for a particular loan, there are points, lender fees, and third-party fees. All other costs, including prepaids, are irrelevant to your selection of a mortgage provider.
- Compare offers by selecting the same rate for each lender and determine the total cost for each. The lender with the best price will have the loan with the lowest total fees for the selected rate. Pay for recurring closing costs out of your pocket—there's no need to finance costs you'd pay for even if you hadn't refinanced.
- Obtain documentation for any price changes and request your HUD-1 settlement statement be delivered the day before your loan closes. If there are any unwarranted

changes, don't proceed with the closing until they have been resolved.

- Don't be fooled by advertising schemes that sound exclusive or too good to be true. There's almost always a hitch. These lenders don't deserve your attention.

Nothing about the MYOM Shopping System is based upon the payment—it's based upon the price. Keep this concept at the forefront and you'll save yourself a lot of grief.

Remember the law protects you—use it to your advantage. Review the information in chapter 11 before you shop.

Mastering the shopping process is only part of the equation—you must also actively monitor your mortgage debt, refinancing only when it's beneficial to do so. Managing your mortgage is a process that will continue for as long as you have one; and the more you know about it, the earlier you'll become mortgage free.

Manage It

Minding your mortgage means managing it. You must stay focused on the end result: becoming mortgage free. This means you must do the following:

- Use the MYOM Shopping System.
- Gain the proper perspective of home ownership.
- Take control of your monthly spending decisions.
- Deploy a sound refinance strategy.

Specifically, you need to:

1. Own your home—don't let it own you.

Besides the obvious need for shelter and the desire to provide for your family, the primary reasons to own a home are to:

- Provide a hedge against inflation
- Provide long-term asset appreciation

The former is achieved by using only fixed-rate mortgage products. You'll be protected from the rising cost of housing since your payment will be fixed, and you'll provide a baseline from which to further reduce the cost of housing by employing sound refinance strategies.

The latter is accomplished when you choose to pay down your mortgage debt, which creates equity in addition to the increase in the value of your home. That equity is protected by way of your inflation-proof payment, which will remain stable regardless of economic conditions.

2. Convert your monthly spending decisions into wealth

Your monthly discretionary spending is financed by your debt. Each time you decide to spend rather than to pay down your mortgage, it costs you time and money, because paying down your mortgage accelerates the payoff date (time), and because paying down your mortgage cancels interest charges on a compounding basis (money).

When you make a curtailment (paying down additional principal) of any kind, you initiate the mortgage snowball. Once you set it in motion, it gains size in the form of interest savings and speed in the form of an accelerated payoff date. This phenomenon is based on the following cycle that starts with the first curtailment:

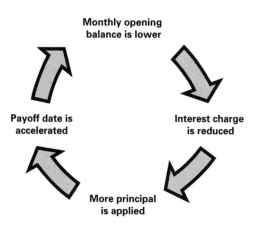

**Monthly opening
balance is lower**

**Payoff date is
accelerated**

**Interest charge
is reduced**

**More principal
is applied**

The Mortgage Snowball Cycle

This cycle repeats itself in "layers" for each additional principal payment made. Since it's circular, each layer feeds off itself, racking up compounded interest savings and further accelerating the payoff date.

Dramatic results are attainable—they can reduce your mortgage term by at least one-third without much effort.

Because your payment does not change, you must overcome the need for instant gratification. You must take a stand against the culture and focus on paying down your debt. Be patient. The mortgage snowball might begin the size of a baseball, but as soon as it gains momentum, it'll grow to massive proportions.

Think about this: the mustard seed is the smallest of all, yet it grows to the largest of all garden plants. Don't be led astray by thinking an extra $50 isn't going to make a difference—it will. Start with a small commitment if that's all you can muster. Once you get into the habit, you'll find it easier to add more to your monthly mortgage payment and you'll eventually move your mountain of debt.

The Mortgage Minder Dashboard, available by logging on to www.mindyourownmortgage.com, will give you the tools you need to set up and monitor your personal progress in becoming mortgage free. You can perform "what if" analyses, monitor the impact of making curtailments, view your cumulative interest savings, and see your early payoff date. If you use the tool consistently, you will develop the necessary habits to facilitate significant progress.

3. Deploy a sound refinance strategy.

If you allow the mortgage industry to ping you whenever they believe you should refinance, you are asking for trouble. You must deploy the MYOM Refinance Strategy:

- Refinance only when you can accomplish all three objectives: lower the cost of your mortgage, accelerate the payoff date, and ensure you surpass break-even on total fees and anything else added to the new loan balance.
- Use the MYOM Shopping System and find the best deals.
- Keep it simple by sticking to fixed-rate loans.
- Never take cash out.

Deploying the MYOM Refinance Strategy will allow you to think about a refinance in the following manner:

- Your current lender offers to change your rate, requiring you to continue to make your regular payment.
- Your current lender charges you a fee to obtain the rate, not to lower your payment.

The only difference between this concept and the real world is that you aren't required to make the old payment when you refinance into a new loan. Applying this new line of thinking, however, enables you to make sound refinance decisions that will make significant contributions to your early payoff date.

Combining the refinance strategy with making additional principal payments on a regular basis will result in exponential savings. The interaction of interest-rate reductions and contributions to principal supercharge the equation. Given the right market conditions, it's not unreasonable to expect to cut your mortgage cost and payoff date in half.

Finish It

You've discovered an entirely new way to think about mortgage debt. Now go use what you have learned and make the necessary moves to eliminate it as quickly as possible.

There is no better time than now to take advantage of the principles taught in this book. Interest rates are at historic lows, and if you qualify for a sound refinance, it would be foolish not to take action.

If you hold an adjustable-rate mortgage, don't wait. Interest rates are sure to increase rapidly in the next several years once the inevitable inflationary cycle begins. Trade that ticking time bomb for the security of a fixed-rate loan.

The pain caused by the credit crisis and the ensuing economic meltdown is rooted in our economy's dependency on high levels of consumer spending that leaves no room for savings at the household level. Credit, whether or not it's as free-flowing as it was before the crash, is to be avoided at all costs. Stick with housing and transportation and leave it at that. Never let your home become the source of financing for a lifestyle you can't afford. You can be sure there will be a return to consumerism. Don't participate!

It doesn't make sense to depend on the government or anyone else to straighten things out in your household. You need to take the economic bull by the horns. It's time to create some stimulus of your own:

- Shop right—Don't get stuck with overcharges or the wrong loan. Use the MYOM Shopping System and force the lenders to show their cards.
- Take action—With a renewed focus on your monthly spending, you can get started right away. Start making those additional principal payments. Eliminate future interest charges and accelerate your payoff date.
- Refinance when it benefits you—The MYOM Refinance Strategy will result in home financing that supplements your wealth, rather than detracting from it.

Log onto www.mindyourownmortgage.com today to get started on your personal journey. You'll find all the tools you need to automate the MYOM Shopping System process, manage your mortgage, make sound refinance decisions, and apply the other concepts in this book to your personal financial situation. Go on now—create your own mortgage revolution and break away from the system.

Set yourself apart from the crowd. It's time to make it happen.

A FINAL WORD:
Healing Our Nation

Our nation is in desperate need of healing. That healing begins and ends at the household level: only strong household economies will result in a strong national economy. Economic healing can only occur by building financially viable households, one by one.

This means we can't revert to the old ways. It's impossible to prosper if you live beyond your means. This applies to individuals, families, businesses, and the government. Thus, the culture of consumerism is a trap. We took down the economy because we allowed the free market to take advantage of our weaknesses. That does not, in and of itself, make the free market a bad thing. It's up to us to say no! Spurring another consumer nation that spends at the same irresponsible levels of the past will only defer the inevitable. Building a better America starts in the trenches—with you and me.

This applies to the mortgage industry too. Despite the meltdown, it's operating in much the same way as it was before the crash. The messaging about lower payments—about the monthly "savings"—hasn't changed one bit since the meltdown. And it won't in the near future, but now you know better.

It's time to get serious about creating a sustainable American economy. I've said it before: the moment we begin to live financially responsible lives, the economy will tank. Fortunately, this will be a temporary problem—the system will adapt to a country of savers if we stick to our guns. Consider it a grassroots campaign, starting with being smarter about our largest debt—our mortgages—and extending it into the way we live our lives. We must ignore the prod to spend and take it upon ourselves to stand strong. It's a free market—just as it should be—and we are free to decide.

I hope this book does more than turn the mortgage industry on its head. I hope it inspires you to find your path to financial restoration and stay there, creating a sustainable economy that will benefit generations to come.

ACKNOWLEDGMENTS

This book is a dream come true. For quite some time, I've been aching to get this information out to the mortgage-buying public. Writing a book and attempting to market it during these economic times is no small task. But there were a number of folks who took to heart what I had to say, encouraging me along the way. This, along with many events that could only be explained through divine circumstance, led to the publication of *Mind Your Own Mortgage*.

The concept for this book dates back to my days at E*TRADE Financial, where I had the pleasure to work with a group of people who truly cared about doing right by the consumer. Yet mortgage companies are many times like the Titanic—they gain steam and then the market turns so fast there isn't time to steer the ship from harm. I thank the team members I had the pleasure of working with through each and every challenge—even though E*TRADE's mortgage company ended up a fatality to the market and other forces, you stood strong to the end.

I also want to thank:

Chris Goulard, pastor of stewardship at Saddleback Church, for his leadership and the honor of serving alongside of him. It was through our Financial Freedom workshops that the materials were refined for what became *Mind Your Own Mortgage.*

Betty Hopkins of Saddleback Church, who worked closely and patiently with me to develop the class materials for the workshops, and for her endless support and enthusiasm over this project.

My friends and brothers who encouraged me and held me accountable to get the job done—Pete Todd (who was the first to point me in the right direction), Dave Arnold, Pat Stafford, and Chris Goulard. None of you ever let up on me. Thank you!

My Saddleback Church small group, who my wife and I "do life" with.

Mary Hunt for her wisdom, enthusiasm, great charm, and tenacious desire to help others. I cherish your friendship.

Frank Pastore for taking a chance on me by putting me in his rotation on live L.A. talk radio (no tape delays!). Thank you, Frank, for investing in me and raising my batting average—despite the damage to your ERA.

My pastors, Rick Warren and Kenny Luck, who have been a constant source of inspiration and have fueled my spiritual growth. You have challenged me to walk firmly and strongly in my faith by serving as great men of faith yourselves. Although I blow it often, you always pick me back up with your words of encouragement.

Susan Goetz, who edited the manuscript to ready it for distribution to potential publishers.

Jamie Chavez of WordWorks, who served as editor through to the finished product. You are a professional and can make words sing like no other.

The entire team at Thomas Nelson—a set of truly amazing people who take great care in their work. Gary Davidson, for opening the door to Kristen Parrish, Kristi Henson, Curt Harding, Joel Miller and Kristen Vasgaard. I am humbled that such a fine organization has published this material.

My agent, Bucky Rosenbaum, a wonderful man. I had the good fortune to meet you at what turned out to be impeccable timing. Yet another divine circumstance.

My late friend, Andrew Walin, who at the age of thirty-five went home to be with God after a valiant fight with cancer. You inspired me most of all—not once over years of suffering did I see you give up. And every time we spoke or met, you beat me to the punch by asking how *I* was doing. A brave, humble, and caring person such as you I will not meet again—until we meet again. I love you, pal.

And the best—my lovely wife Kim and my amazing children. You stood behind me and sacrificed much to enable this work. To my parents, Carlo and Ingrid, who laid a foundation of financial responsibility that I rejected as a foolish teen and circled back to after realizing mom and dad were right all along. This book would not be without the support of my loving family.

And most importantly to my rock, without which my life would be built on sand—Jesus Christ. Thank you, God, for your Son!

ABOUT THE AUTHOR

Rob Bernabé is a twenty-five-year veteran of the financial services industry. He began his career at KPMG, advising a wide variety of financial services companies, and later led several prominent mortgage companies, including E*TRADE Mortgage and the restructuring of H&R Block Mortgage. Rob was a pioneer in online mortgage lending, growing E*TRADE Mortgage from a small company to the third-largest online lender in the nation in less than three years. Under Rob's passion for consumer advocacy, E*TRADE shook the mortgage industry by becoming the first to widely offer upfront guaranteed mortgage pricing, and offering the nation's first portable mortgage.

Rob's goal is to create a consumer-led revolution of the mortgage industry. His teaching brings clarity and simplicity to mortgage consumers by placing information in their hands that will empower them to manage, minimize, and eliminate their mortgage debt. He serves on the financial stewardship team at Saddleback Church in Lake Forest, California, and is a frequent speaker on personal finance and life skills.

He lives in Southern California with his wife, two children, and three dachshunds.

INDEX